━━

BECCARIA
On Crimes and Punishments and Other Writings

CAMBRIDGE TEXTS IN THE HISTORY OF POLITICAL THOUGHT

Series editors

RAYMOND GEUSS
Reader in Philosophy, University of Cambridge

QUENTIN SKINNER
Regius Professor of Modern History, University of Cambridge

Cambridge Texts in the History of Political Thought is now firmly established as the major student textbook series in political theory. It aims to make available to students all the most important texts in the history of western political thought, from ancient Greece to the early twentieth century. All the familiar classic texts will be included but the series seeks at the same time to enlarge the conventional canon by incorporating an extensive range of less well-known works, many of them never before available in a modern English edition. Wherever possible, texts are published in complete and unabridged form, and translations are specially commissioned for the series. Each volume contains a critical introduction together with chronologies, biographical sketches, a guide to further reading and any necessary glossaries and textual apparatus. When completed, the series will aim to offer an outline of the entire evolution of western political thought.

For a list of titles published in the series, please see end of book.

BECCARIA

On Crimes and Punishments and Other Writings

EDITED BY

RICHARD BELLAMY

University of East Anglia

AND TRANSLATED BY

RICHARD DAVIES

Instituto di Anglistica, University of Bergamo

WITH

VIRGINIA COX

University of Cambridge

AND

RICHARD BELLAMY

CAMBRIDGE
UNIVERSITY PRESS

CAMBRIDGE UNIVERSITY PRESS
Cambridge, New York, Melbourne, Madrid, Cape Town, Singapore, São Paulo

Cambridge University Press
The Edinburgh Building, Cambridge CB2 8RU, UK

Published in the United States of America by Cambridge University Press, New York

www.cambridge.org
Information on this title: www.cambridge.org/9780521402033

First published 1995
Fourth printing 2003

A catalogue record for this publication is available from the British Library

Library of Congress Cataloguing in Publication data
Beccaria, Cesare, marchese di, 1738–1794.
[Selections. English]
On crimes and punishments, and other writings / Cesare Beccaria;
edited by Richard Bellamy; translated by Richard Davies, Virginia Cox.
p.   cm. – (Cambridge texts in the history of political thought)
Includes bibliographical references (p. xliv) and index.
Contents: On Crimes and Punishments – To Jean Baptiste D'Alembert –
To André Morellet – Inaugural Lecture – Reflections on The
Barbarousness and the Civilisation of Nations and on the Savage
State of Man – Reflections on Manners and Customs – On Luxury.
ISBN 0 521 40203 4 (hardback)
1. Punishment – Early works to 1800. 2. Political science – Early works
to 1800. I. Bellamy, Richard (Richard Paul) II. Davies, Richard
(Richard Brian), 1944– .
III. Cox. Virginia. IV. Title. V. Series.
HV8661.B15213   1995
364.6 – dc20   94-20983   CIP

ISBN 978-0-521-40203-3 hardback
ISBN 978-0-521-47982-0 paperback

Transferred to digital printing 2007

Contents

Contents

Contents

Acknowledgements

Richard Davies provided an initial translation of all the texts, which was subsequently substantially revised first by the editor and then by Virginia Cox of the University of Cambridge. The editor is extremely grateful to Dr Cox for her detailed comments on the translation. Richard Davies also supplied the Biographical glossary and some of the notes to the letters and other writings. All other editorial matter, including the Introduction and the Note on the texts, is the work of the editor.

Introduction

Beccaria's classic study *On Crimes and Punishments* belongs to the category of works which are much cited and little read. In Beccaria's case the reasons for this relative neglect are twofold. First, until recently even those who have attempted to read him, either in the original or in translation, have had to rely on a corrupt text. As is explained in the Note on the texts, the present edition provides the first English version of the book as it was last published and revised by Beccaria. Second, the context provided by Beccaria's other writings and those of his circle is rarely known, so that the background assumptions on which his argument rested have either appeared obscure or simply been misconstrued. As a result, Beccaria has come to be pigeon-holed as one of the founding fathers of a putative tradition of classic penal reformers, and the distinctiveness of his contribution has been recognised only rarely. His argument, however, was more complex than a number of commentators have appreciated, anticipating in an original way some of the solutions and difficulties of contemporary philosophers of punishment.

Punishment forms part of a wider system of social organisation and is sustained by a broad range of social practices, attitudes and institutions. Beccaria's argument for penal reform reflected a whole new discourse about the nature of society and the need for social change more generally, and has to be read as part of this larger movement. Some account of the intellectual, social and political context of Beccaria's activity, therefore, forms a necessary preliminary to any analysis of the text.

Beccaria wrote his treatise whilst a member of a short-lived group of intellectuals known as the Accademia dei pugni, or Academy of Fisticuffs. This society, which lasted from 1762 to 1766, consisted of a small number of young men who regularly met to discuss and study together. Self-consciously modelled on the circle of French *philosophes* gathered around the *Encyclopédie*, they were a far less formal association than the numerous other literary societies and academies that abounded in Italy at this time. The name was adopted by Pietro Verri, their prime mover, when he learned that their discussions had the reputation of becoming so heated that they ended up in a fight. Between 1764 and 1766, members of the 'academy' also published the periodical *Il caffe* as a means of disseminating their ideas.

Although their interests were wide-ranging, their activity was essentially centred on winning over the Austrian rulers of Lombardy to a broad programme of reform and to bringing attention to themselves as potential agents of these changes within the imperial administration. The Habsburgs had held Lombardy since 1707, but did not begin the process of reform until the end of the War of the Austrian Succession in 1748. The initial impetus in Lombardy, as elsewhere, was the need to improve the administration of finances and the economy in order to reduce the massive deficit created by the cost of war. As Beccaria indicated in his inaugural lecture as Professor of Cameral Sciences, the most significant element of the reform programme was the completion of a new land register, the *catasto*. Begun in the 1740s, it was completed by the Florentine official Pompeo Neri in 1757. Outlining his aims in an important report in 1750, which set the agenda for all later reforms, Neri had proposed the abolition of all taxes except for those on land and the removal of all the exemptions allowed to nobles and the Church. The new register also offered an opportunity for redrawing the provincial and district boundaries, a review of the methods employed for the collection of taxes and a reappraisal of customs tariffs.

These measures brought the Habsburg regime into conflict with the Lombard establishment, for they threatened the independence and privileges of Church, patriciate and aristocracy. These groups resisted the reforms through numerous legal battles and appeals to precedent. Initially these countermeasures had some success.

However, the further deterioration of state finances due to the Seven Years War of 1756–63 gave a fresh stimulus to the reorganisation of the province and its integration into the political structure of the Empire. In 1759 a new impetus was given to the reform movement by the appointment of Count Carlo di Firmian, whom Beccaria came to regard as his protector as minister plenipotentiary. Supported by the Austrian Minister of Foreign Affairs, Count Kaunitz, the next decade witnessed a concerted attack on ecclesiastical powers and immunities and the undermining of the position of local notables.

Beccaria's and his colleagues' writings belong to this second phase. Members of the ruling aristocracy, they nevertheless rejected the juridical mentality of their parents. Pietro Verri's clash with his father was particularly emblematic of this generational conflict. Gabrielle Verri had played an important part in the counter-attack of the Milanese establishment against the incursions of the Austrian government, defending in a series of works the local legal and administrative traditions of the Lombard region. Pietro, however, bitterly criticised the antiquarian and jurisprudential culture that then predominated in Milan and placed all state affairs in the hands of lawyers and scholars. Unlike either his brother Alessandro or Beccaria, he never took a legal degree. Instead, he escaped to fight in the Seven Years War. When in 1761, after an unsuccessful attempt to seek employment in Vienna, he returned to Milan, it was as a champion of the very reforms his father was attempting to block.

When Verri renewed his acquaintance with Beccaria in 1761 he found a willing disciple. Born in 1738, the eldest son of a reasonably wealthy noble family, Beccaria had become similarly estranged from his parents due to their attempts to prevent his marriage to Teresa Blasco, whom they considered socially inferior. As he confessed in his letter to André Morellet, reproduced below, his 'philosophical conversion' to the writings of the French Enlightenment dated from this period (p. 122). Rousseau's recently published *La Nouvelle Héloïse*, in particular, offered a new discourse of moral sensibility that echoed his own romantic temperament and concerns. His first child, born in 1762, was symbolically named Giulia, after Julie – the heroine of the novel. Encouraged by Verri, in whose house he and his wife found temporary refuge, Beccaria's conflict with his family developed into a thoroughgoing critique of the values and social system that underlay their opposition. The passages in *On Crimes* dealing with parental tyranny are only the most obvious indicators of the links Beccaria made between the organisation of the family and that of society as a whole. Like Verri, his aim became the substitution of the existing irregular, particularist and custom-bound legal system, based on hereditary rights and the personal rule of the monarch and nobility, by a regular, centralised and rational system of justice that was equal for all and grounded in the rule of law.

Against the traditionalist thinking of the lawyers and the Church, Verri, Beccaria and their circle placed the developing languages of political economy and of a secular morality that sought to harness and cultivate, rather than to repress, the passions. Verri's writings on these subjects provide the necessary starting point for any consideration of Beccaria's thought. For Beccaria's ideas largely developed through daily discussion of his friend's views. Indeed, as the Note on the text shows, Verri played a major role in initiating and eventually editing Beccaria's most important work.

Whilst in Vienna, Verri had drafted his *Elements of Commerce*, which he later published in *Il caffe*. This treatise reflected the neo-mercantilism of writers such as Melon and Forbonnais, who tempered their advocacy of *laissez-faire* with a continuing role for the state, particularly in fostering domestic manufacturing industry, and a general concern to discourage foreign imports in order to secure a favourable national trade balance. Although he later modified the protectionist aspects of his views, ultimately favouring the abandonment of all restrictive practices such as guilds or the granting of monopolies for example, Verri remained largely indifferent to physiocratic ideas. He argued that stimulating the manufacturing and the export market would bring about an increase in agricultural production and a rise in population of their own accord. More in tune with the advanced economic theories of the time were his ideas on luxury and equality. Here Verri followed David Hume in believing that luxury provided a necessary incentive for work and industrial innovation, both creating wealth and destroying privilege in the process by forcing landowners to dissipate their wealth in conspicuous consumption, and with it their economic power. To foster further the breakdown of feudal ties, he advocated the abolition of *fidecommessi*, entails and other special rights of nobility that restricted the exchange of property and the free movement of labour. He contended that the commercial system not only required a more formally egalitarian society, in which there were no social barriers to freedom of contract and to trade, but led to the resulting prosperity being more equally distributed as well. Verri also shared Hume's conception of money as a universal commodity that oiled the wheels of commerce by providing a uniform medium of exchange, and had corresponding worries about the dangers of paper credit and inflation. As the extracts reproduced below indicate, Beccaria's lectures of 1769–70, posthumously published as *Elements of Public Economy*, developed substantially similar arguments.

Verri's programme fitted with the interventionist tendencies of the Habsburg regime and their central concern with increasing state revenue. Even the egalitarian aspect of Verri's thought found an echo in the Austrians' desire to dismantle those privileges of the *ancien régime* which stood in the way of the process of centralisation and reform. The earliest publications of the group gathered around Verri were concerned with championing particular economic and fiscal policies associated with his theories. Verri began his campaign with an essay on the salt tax (1761) and from 1762–3 was engaged in composing his extensive *Considerations on the Commerce of the State of Milan*, in which he provided a comprehensive analysis of the decline of Lombard trade and the need to revive it through legal reform, internal free trade and the abolition of the tax farm. Beccaria's first publication was a pamphlet *On the Monetary Disorders and their Remedies in the State of Milan in 1762*, in which he employed his skills as a mathematician to advocate the need for a stable rate of exchange in preference to Milan adopting its own currency as the best means of facilitating trade. Running through all these proposals was a desire to reduce the laws regulating trade to a more systematic order that reflected the rational economic calculations of individuals rather than a complex pattern of entrenched traditions, privileges and special interests. Both Verri and Beccaria were able to fashion powerful criticisms of the existing system with these new analytical tools. Beccaria's brief essay on smuggling of 1764, for instance, offered a classic early application of the mathematical formulation of rational choice theory in order to quantify how high tariffs could be before contraband proved worthwhile. Although many of their specific suggestions were ignored, the activity of these reformers brought them to sufficient prominence for the Austrian government ultimately to place many of them in important positions within the Lombard administration. Both Verri (in 1765) and Beccaria (from 1771), for example, ended up on the Supreme Council of the Economy, a body that had been in part created in response to their ideas.

Underlying these economic proposals, with their attack on feudal attitudes and practices, was a new account of human motivation and morals. The link between economics, ethics and psychology was provided by the concept of happiness – the subject of Verri's *Meditations on Happiness* of 1763, which was published shortly before Beccaria's treatise on punishment, and at the time was occasionally attributed to him. Giuseppe Ricuperati has called this book, rather than Beccaria's more famous work, the true 'manifesto of the Accademia dei pugni'. Enunciating a conception of legitimacy that was to be fundamental to Beccaria's argument, Verri declared that 'The end of the social pact is the well-being of each of the individuals who join together to form society, who do so in order that this well-being becomes absorbed into the public happiness or rather the greatest possible happiness distributed with the greatest equality possible.' In accordance with the lessons of the new political economy, the maximisation of public wealth and happiness required the equal protection of individuals. Behind his qualified utilitarian goal lay a hedonistic psychology and associationist epistemology principally derived, albeit with important modifications, from Locke, Helvétius and Condillac. Verri shared the contemporary view that the passions were the springs of human action. However, he continued to accord reason a decisive role in the refinement and direction of our passional urges. Moreover, he treated the flight from pain rather than the pursuit of pleasure *per se* as the decisive factor. Happiness, therefore, consisted of more than the passing enjoyment of mere pleasurable sensations. Rather, it was achieved through the rational pursuit of our interests through the removal of obstacles to our well-being, such as poverty. In this way, the spread of ideas or enlightenment and the programme of economic and social reform came together, with the one producing the other and promoting in the process the progressive civilisation of society by providing for the greater satisfaction and refinement of human needs.

Similar assumptions underlay Beccaria's writings. His study of crimes and punishments has often been treated as narrowly focussed on the issue of penal reform. Even Verri, who grew jealous at the fame the work brought his 25-year-old protégé, was apt to dismiss it as a limited exercise that he had set his young companion in applying the reformer's ideas to a specific problem. The book was much more ambitious, however. Beccaria sought to establish a legal framework that reflected the general programme of the reformers to replace the existing system of semi-feudal privileges, customs and honours with a new conception of social organisation, based on a regular system of justice involving equal laws for all. This project was intimately connected to the academy's understanding of human nature and their views on political economy, which furnished him with the principles that guided his work. His purpose was to make punishment the chief instrument of reform by leading human beings, via their reason and passions, to the progressive promotion of the public happiness. As we shall see, however, Beccaria conceived this proposal in essentially liberal terms, as requiring the state to allow individuals to pursue their happiness in their own way so long as they did not harm others in the process.

As Beccaria made clear in his prefatory note To the Reader, appended to the fifth edition in reply to his critics, his aim was to provide an entirely secular account of the origins and function of law. He studiously avoided appeals to either revelation or natural law, making a clear distinction between God's justice, which was best left to Him, and terrestrial justice. The foundation of Beccaria's theory was human nature and in particular 'ineradicable human sentiments' (p. 10). Beccaria shared Verri's positive evaluation of the function of pain. Whilst he believed 'pleasure and pain are the motive forces of all sentient beings', he thought 'every act of our will is always proportional to the strength of the sensory impression that gives rise to it' (pp. 21, 41). As he later specified, this meant that 'the proximate and efficient cause of actions is the flight from pain, their final cause is the love of pleasure', since 'man rests in good times and acts when in pain' (p. 157). Indeed, in his *Elements of Public Economy* (1769) he maintained that even the prospect of pleasure or of greater utility acted upon us only indirectly, via the pain resulting from the anxiety associated with the possibility of its not being achieved (p. 163). In this way, Beccaria was able to avoid one of the classic dilemmas confronting a social ethic based on a hedonistic psychology – namely, the worry that people will prefer either a very low level of contentment or base pleasures to the struggle to achieve quantitatively and qualitatively higher levels of fulfilment. On his view, we can never be fully satisfied. We are continuously driven on by the fear of being deprived of our present pleasures combined with a constant dissatisfaction with those pleasures created by the possibility of there being even greater pleasures to be attained. The resulting continual expansion of human needs was at the heart of his account of the progress of society, explaining the development of commerce through the multiplication of luxury goods as well as the role of law.

Beccaria followed the empiricist argument of Locke and Helvétius in attributing all human knowledge, including morality, to the operation of impressions upon our senses. However, he did not interpret this process in a totally mechanistic or deterministic manner. In common with Verri, he retained an element of the rationalist view in attributing a distinct function to human reason in the ordering and synthesising of our sense impressions. Moreover, far from reason being the slave of the passions, as in Hume, both the Italians believed that the distinctiveness of human beings lay in their capacity to control and channel them rationally. Civilisation resulted from the cultivation of this capacity. The spread of ideas or enlightenment became in this way directly related to the promotion of reform (see *On Crimes*, chapter 42).

This modified empiricist epistemology provided the basis for Beccaria's attempt to place the law on what he regarded as a more rational footing. In general terms, law had to be clear and punishment speedy, certain and an economical deterrent so as to ensure an indisputable association of ideas between pain and crime. A rational legal system required that laws be as precise as possible, with judicial discretion reduced to a minimum, so that all citizens knew where they stood and could reason accordingly.

This approach, though present to some degree in Helvétius, was to become very influential, especially through the work of Jeremy Bentham, who found Beccaria's work extremely suggestive. Bentham credited him with being 'the father of *Censorial Jurisprudence*' – the first thinker to attempt a critical or 'censorial', as opposed to a merely expository, account of the law, which sought to demystify and correct the prejudices and confused reasoning that guided most contemporary legal decision making. Indeed, Beccaria provided Bentham with one of his most important tools of criticism. For Beccaria not only followed Locke in seeking to analyse complex ideas into their simple, experience related parts. As H. L. A. Hart has observed, he also anticipated Bentham's elaboration of this technique in order to deconstruct the supposed logical fictions that in their eyes constituted the bulk of our traditional legal and moral concepts. Both thinkers appreciated that terms such as 'right', 'duty' and 'obligation' could not be defined readily in terms of concrete material objects and their effects upon us. As Beccaria put it, such words were 'abbreviated symbols of a rational argument and not of an idea' (p. 12). It was necessary, therefore, to look not for definitions of these words alone but of the complete sentence or argument within which they were employed. Only then would it be possible to translate such statements into others in which the words to be explained did not appear and were replaced instead by things which could be directly experienced and analysed in terms of pleasure and pain – a procedure Bentham called *paraphrasis*. For both thinkers, notions of obligation and of duties, which lay behind doctrines of rights, were all abbreviations for the argument that we will suffer a sanction unless we behave in a particular way. As a result, our basic legal and political vocabulary boiled down to the possibility of punishment or the infliction of pain if we do not act in a stipulated manner. The establishment of the right to punish, therefore, provided the key to our understanding of the whole legal and political system and consequently was the starting point for Beccaria's theory.

Beccaria agreed with Hobbes that the asocial state was one of war, and that fear and the desire for security provided the motivation for uniting to form society. Characteristically, it was the prospect of pain rather than of pleasure that moved us to act. However, he was far from believing that we sacrificed all our liberty to the Leviathan in return for the protection it offered us. On the contrary, he contended that we give up only the smallest portion of our liberty, i.e. that portion necessary for us to enjoy the remaining part in peace and tranquillity (p. 11). As a result, law was justified only to the extent that it was limited to what was required to preserve the maximal amount of individual liberty possible.

Beccaria employed the idea of a social contract more as a theoretical device for setting limits to the legitimacy of law than as an actual historical act to explain its origins. However, in the same chapter he made reference to a classic utilitarian justification for law. If there were a sufficiently large secondary literature on Beccaria to contain interpretative disputes, this combination of contractarian and utilitarian arguments would no doubt have given rise to 'the Beccaria problem'. For it is generally argued that the utilitarian argument either negates the contractarian or renders it unnecessary and vice versa. On the one hand, utilitarians have tended to regard the notion of a social contract as either redundant or a pernicious fiction. If the purpose of government is to secure optimal welfare then our obligation to obey any law lasts so long as it performs this function better than any alternative and no longer. Contractarian notions of consent and related considerations of natural rights seem beside the point and merely serve to help individuals withdraw their support for the general good. On the other hand, social contract theorists have suggested that utilitarianism fails to show a sufficient degree of equality of concern and respect for the differences between individuals. They accuse utilitarians of potentially sacrificing the individual to the greater good of society as a whole. From their perspective, the contract argument appears as a way of ensuring that individuals are not used as a means for some collective purpose.

The seeming confusion arising from Beccaria's mixture of these apparently conflicting arguments draws additional plausibility from the fact that the first English translation of Beccaria's book wrongly credited its author with making 'the greatest happiness of the greatest number' the benchmark of all laws and other human arrangements. In the hands of Bentham, this principle became the sole foundation of morals and legislation and was employed by him in a merciless attack on all contractarian and rights-based arguments. However, although Bentham owed the wording of his formula – if not the ideas behind it – to this source, and in spite of the fact that all subsequent English translators have continued to attribute it to Beccaria, the Italian never employed the phrase. His exact words were 'the greatest (*massima*) happiness shared among the greater (*maggior*) number'.

Unfortunately, even this formulation offers a poor guide to Beccaria's meaning. The notion of division might suggest that he had in mind average as opposed to aggregate utility, whilst the use of the comparative (*maggior*) instead of the superlative (*massima*) potentially indicates that he might have meant 'the greatest happiness of the majority' rather than of the 'largest number'. However, Beccaria's discussion of the utilitarian injunction elsewhere reveals that such inferences would be wrong and that his own wording here is also misleading and imprecise. In these other passages, it becomes clear that his meaning is much closer to that expressed by Verri in his *Meditazioni*, cited above, who together with Hutcheson, Helvétius, and (less directly) Bacon and Rousseau inspired his thesis. From these sources, it emerges that Beccaria was concerned to maximise equally the happiness of each person – a goal he shared not just with Verri but with other members of the *Caffè* group. Thus, in the *Fragment on Smells* (1764) he defines the public good as 'the greatest sum of pleasures, divided equally amongst the greatest number of people', whilst in his *Reflections on the Barbarousness and Civilisation of Nations and on the Savage State of Man* he went so far as to describe 'barbarity' as a disequilibrium between knowledge and opinion, on the one hand, and 'each individual's needs and greatest expectations of happiness', on the other. More importantly, in his *Elements of Public Economy* he defined the sovereign as the 'just and equitable distributor of public happiness' and this latter as 'the happiness of all those individuals that are subject to him'. Consequently, he included amongst his list of 'false ideas of utility', enumerated in chapter 40 of *On Crimes*, any attempt 'to give a multitude of sensible beings the symmetry and order of brute inanimate matter' or doctrines that 'separate the public good from the good of each individual' (pp. 101–2).

There can be no doubt, then, that Beccaria took both the contractarian and the utilitarian aspects of his doctrine seriously and sought to combine them. Was this synthesis confused, as Bentham's remarks about Beccaria's 'false sources' and 'obscure notions' lead one to believe he thought? Or can a coherent thread be found that links the two into a form of contractarian utilitarianism, in which the good of the individual cannot be sacrificed to the common good? The general drift of Beccaria's theory suggests that he attempted the latter, anticipating in the process a number of arguments more usually associated with Bentham's most famous disciple and critic, J. S. Mill.

Like Mill, Beccaria contended that human welfare was tied up with the protection of certain basic interests, most particularly the security of person and possessions. The moral justification for protecting these interests, however, did not depend upon notions of natural right. Their basis lay in considerations of utility, as being essential to human life and the pursuit of happiness. Moreover, when individual interests came into conflict utility again became the benchmark for resolving these clashes. Indeed, such reasoning underpinned Beccaria's understanding of the moral foundations of the state. Beccaria contended that our interests could not be guaranteed without the legal sanctions and regulatory mechanisms provided by government. However, as we saw, he believed that the agreement to obey the law involved a trade-off, whereby individuals sacrificed a part of their liberty to preserve the greatest possible liberty over all. Both the purpose and limits of government, therefore, were set by what Beccaria regarded as the utilitarian goal of securing the greatest possible happiness of each and every citizen. For to achieve this utilitarian goal we had to submit to a number of general rules which applied equally to all and which were upheld by some authoritative power. The idea of the social contract became in this way both a means for expressing the central utilitarian concern that in minimising pain and maximising pleasure we show equal respect for the interests of each individual and a device for justifying our obligation to uphold this maxim. On this view, the only laws we could and should agree to were those concerned with the furtherance of human well-being, the most vital of which were those prohibiting harm to our vital interests. As a consequence, the only rights that either state or citizen might validly claim flowed from their mutual obligation to preserve those human interests necessary to the reduction of pain and the promotion of happiness.

Beccaria's mixture of contractarianism and utilitarianism served therefore to modify the latter in two main respects. First, the contract established that the purpose of government was to govern according to rules that promoted the public happiness by giving the greatest possible protection to the vital interests of each and every citizen rather than by pursuing the greatest possible aggregate utility. Although it is not clear that Beccaria appreciated that his attempt to equalise happiness might conflict with his desire to maximise happiness, forced to choose between the two he invariably opted for the former rather than the latter. Second, by making the rules subject to a contract, Beccaria effectively blocked the collapse of rule into act utilitarianism, which would have allowed the government to weigh each case on its particular merits. Both these moves served to prevent the utilitarian reasoning which he employed as an effective tool of social criticism and reform being used in certain instances to sacrifice the individual to the common good. These considerations were of the utmost importance for Beccaria's theory of punishment. They enabled him to escape some of the problems associated with purely utilitarian theories of economical deterrence and to adopt a compromise theory, not dissimilar to that proposed by contemporary philosophers such as John Rawls and H. L. A. Hart, which found room for the concerns of retributivists as well.

Very briefly, the respective merits and demerits of the retributive and utilitarian views of punishment have been traditionally described as follows. For the utilitarian, punishment is forward-looking. Its basic purpose is the reduction of crimes, and hence pain, in the future. From this perspective, past wrongs cannot be undone, merely prevented from reoccurring by making illegal actions less attractive than legal ones. For the retributivist, in contrast, punishment is backward-looking. It follows from guilt and aims to ensure that wrongdoers suffer in proportion to their wrongdoing. Retributivists have made two general and related criticisms of the utilitarian view, both of which strike at the heart of Beccaria's theory. First, they claim that utilitarianism might lead to the imposition of excessive punishments for relatively minor offences. For the gain to society resulting from deterring multiple minor infractions of the law by administering a severe exemplary punishment, such as hanging some one for double parking, might outweigh the pain caused to the unfortunate individuals selected to be made an example of. Second, they have argued that utilitarianism could even justify punishing an innocent person for a crime they did not commit: for example, if the real criminal could not be apprehended and a conviction was necessary to prevent people losing faith in the effectiveness of the forces of law and order and a consequent lessening of the deterrent effect of punishment. Indeed, they contend that utilitarianism creates no *necessary* connection between guilt and punishment at all, other than the rather tenuous link established by the likely undermining of the whole deterrent argument if people come to believe that individuals are simply punished arbitrarily. Utilitarians, in their turn, argue that the retributivist view is circular and vague, amounting to little more than the assertion that someone deserves to be punished because they deserve it. Such theories may be good at specifying who should be punished, namely the transgressor, but are less compelling at explaining why or how. The classic retributivist argument of the *lex talionis* (i.e. 'an eye for an eye, a tooth for a tooth'), for example, proves rather imprecise when it comes to concrete cases. It is unclear, for instance, what form of punishment it decrees for a toothless person who has knocked out someone else's teeth.

Beccaria was well aware of the pros and cons of each of these theories of punishment, and in framing his own theory aimed to draw on the former whilst avoiding the latter. His basic justification for why we should punish was utilitarian. One of the central points of his essay was that the existing system of criminal justice, which was essentially retributive in character, was far too arbitrary and often pointless. Essentially orientated around the *lex talionis*, its basic rationale was that crimes against the body politic should be punished by heaping suffering upon the body of the criminal. Beccaria ridiculed such notions as both useless and unjust. 'Can the wailings of a wretch', he asked, 'undo what has been done and turn back the clock?' Against such views, he asserted that there could be no other purpose for punishment than 'to prevent the offender from doing fresh harm to his fellows and to deter others from doing likewise. Therefore, punishments and the means adopted for inflicting them should, consistent with proportionality, be so selected as to make the most efficacious and lasting impression on the minds of men with the least possible torment to the body of the condemned.' (p. 31).

As we have seen, however, it is precisely at this point, when considerations of whom and how one should punish enter the discussion, that the utilitarian begins to get into difficulties. Beccaria clearly wanted to avoid these problems, since his two other main concerns in the book were that the present system frequently convicted the wrong person and that it exacted unduly harsh penalties. His solution was to introduce some of the retributivist arguments into his theory in ways that paralleled his contractarian view of utilitarianism. His argument was essentially that whilst the basic purpose and rationale of punishment was utilitarian, its application had to be limited by retributivist considerations of guilt. For the contractarian justification that Beccaria gave for the adoption of the utilitarian rules provided by the state, made them subject to the limitation that they afforded each of us equal mutual protection of our basic interests except in those circumstances where we intentionally broke the agreement.

As a result of this dual perspective on punishment, Beccaria made a similar distinction to that proposed by Rawls and Hart between the functions of the legislator and those of the judiciary (pp. 12, 14–15). The first should adopt utilitarian criteria for the framing of laws and punishments, the second employ retributive criteria when applying these rules to particular cases. Moreover, as Foucault has noted, the contractarian argument also enabled Beccaria to distinguish between the public and the private spheres, restricting state action to the former. The legal rules merely operated as an external framework to regulate our social interaction, leaving us as much as possible to pursue our own affairs as we pleased. Punishment referred solely to the restitution of the legal order and to the legal personality of the criminal. Unlike later penal reformers, he did not aim at the rehabilitation of the criminal's moral personality as such (pp. 22–3, 74).

The power of the sovereign to punish offenders, therefore, only became a right to the extent that it was exercised in a manner 'most useful to the greatest number', whilst punishments were only just in so far as they did not go beyond what was necessary 'to unite together particular interests' and prevent society degenerating into a harmful state of warlike anarchy (p. 11). However, what utility entailed was not left to the sovereign's discretion, but was determined by those laws that could have been agreed to under a social contract between free and equal individuals as providing for the greatest possible reduction of harm divided amongst the greatest possible number. Two important consequences followed from these criteria. First, punishment only became justified to the extent that the crime harmed society, the punishment was proportionate to that harm and the individual to be punished had violated the terms of the contract from which everyone benefited. Second, and far more radically, he contended that if the benefits of the legal system failed to be equitably distributed, so that the law promoted the happiness of some rather more than others, then it would not only justify but positively promote crime. In so arguing, Beccaria not only had the privileges and immunities of the Church and nobility in mind, but also the maldistribution of property which gave rise to them. In such circumstances, he argued, it was entirely understandable that the poor should seek to 'break those bonds which are so deadly for the majority and useful only to a handful of indolent tyrants' by returning to a 'natural state of independence' in which, as members of a robber band, they could, for a time at least, 'live free and happy by the fruits of courage and industry' (p. 69). As Venturi has observed, Beccaria moved at this point beyond reform and towards the discourse of utopia. It is little wonder that the term socialism was first coined in Italian by Ferdinando Facchinei, who intended it as a term of abuse, in his critique of Beccaria of 1765.

The best way to illustrate Beccaria's compromise theory is by examining two of his most famous arguments – his case against torture (in *On Crimes*, chapter 16) and, for contemporaries the most original of all, his rejection of the death penalty (in *On Crimes*, chapter 28). Beccaria considered two different uses of torture. First, he examined the practice of judicial torture to get the criminal to confess to his or her crime. Beccaria objected that this procedure was both unjust and inefficient. It was unjust for largely contractarian reasons. Torture involved punishing someone before they had been proven guilty. However, Beccaria argued, society had a duty to protect the individual until it had been 'decided that he had violated the pacts according to which this protection was provided' (p. 39). In other words, we had only submitted to abiding by the laws of the state to the extent that they offered us protection and any attempt to go beyond this remit was illegitimate. He condemned torture as inefficient, though, on largely utilitarian grounds. For a start, he saw no purpose in forcing some one to confess to crimes that could not be proven in some other way, since such offences would presumably be otherwise unknown and hence offered no bad example to others from which they had to be deterred. Even more importantly, though, torture undermined the deterrent effect of punishment. The weak, he claimed, would reason that they could be made to confess to any crime under torture and, on the principle that one might as well be hanged for a sheep as for a lamb, would have no incentive not to commit crimes. The strong, in contrast, would reason that they could withstand the pain and hence could break the law with impunity.

Both the internal evolution of judicial procedure and the impact of the empirical methods of the natural sciences on rules of evidence, a theme Beccaria developed elsewhere in his treatise, had made these latter arguments against torture relatively commonplace. More novel was his case against the second use of torture, as a means of punishment for exonerating guilt. Here he employed the utilitarian reasoning that provided his basic justification of punishment to condemn the retributive use of torture as a means for removing the taint of infamy as pointless and so illegitimate. However, this argument had its dangers since utilitarian theorists of deterrence could be accused, as we saw, of a potential willingness to employ overly severe punishments to achieve their goal, in which case cruel and unusual punishments might be thought occasionally appropriate. Once again, therefore, Beccaria had to adopt a mixture of contractarian and utilitarian reasoning.

In fact, utilitarians can avoid the most simplistic versions of this charge by stressing that their goal is economic deterrence. In other words, they seek to use the least pain possible so as to maximise happiness over all. In general, this criterion entails that punishment is proportionate to the gravity, or harmfulness, of the offence. Beccaria certainly took this view, arguing that crimes ought to be categorised by the harm they inflicted on society and punished accordingly. He insisted that punishments should never be more painful than was necessary to prevent a given crime or outweigh in suffering the harm done to society by the misdemeanour they aimed to prevent. He also believed it important to ensure that criminals had an incentive to commit a lesser rather than a greater crime. Torture, he maintained, was too inflexible and rarely, if ever, possessed these necessary features. In spite of all the ingenuity that had gone into the devising of tortures, their adaptability was limited by the human frame, which could only stand so much. His condemnation of torture for being simply too crude drew additional support from his belief that the duration of a punishment had a greater effect on other people than its intensity. Hard labour lasted over many years, for example, whilst it was difficult to prolong torture for more than a few hours or days without losing your victim. As a result, he doubted that tortures could ever be sufficiently refined so as to provide the carefully graded scale of punishments required by his deterrence argument for punishment to be legitimate. Moreover, he also maintained that torture was essentially brutal and brutalising and as such was likely to increase violent crimes by desensitising people to cruelty.

Nevertheless, such thinking does not rule out torture on principle. Some of his arguments are empirically debatable. Torture, for example, might be prolonged and refined by administering it at weekly intervals rather than at one go. Nor does his case exclude the possibility that the cumulative effect of some minor but common crime could justify on utilitarian grounds a harsher penalty in order to stamp it out than a rare but grave offence. It does not even ensure that some barbarous penalty inflicted on an innocent person might not be allowable in certain rare instances, although we have already noted Beccaria's separate argument against this possibility. To prevent such exemplary punishments ever being justified, however unlikely they might be, Beccaria had to turn once again to the contractarian argument underlying his utilitarianism, whereby the utilitarian strategy was adopted as a means for giving equal weight and protection to the interests of every individual. According to this line of argument, although it might in some highly hypothetical case make sense to convict and torture a relatively innocuous person, it could never make good utilitarian sense to institute such a practice by giving the state the right to do so. In the language of modern utilitarianism, the contract bound the state to follow certain utilitarian rules rather than to weigh up all actions on the basis of utilitarian criteria. For to allow any institution to do the latter involves handing over a wide degree of arbitrary power the utility of which is highly doubtful.

This move becomes clearer in Beccaria's discussion of the death penalty. Beccaria believed that the most novel feature of his argument was the utilitarian claim that the death penalty could never have been established because to give the state the right to kill its members on a regular basis, even subject to numerous limiting conditions, could never be deemed useful or necessary to the protection of their interests. As with his argument against torture, the main part of this reasoning related to his belief that the death penalty was essentially wasteful and a doubtful deterrent. He argued that by killing the criminal, a potentially useful member of society who could have repaid his or her debt to society was taken out of circulation. Moreover, he believed that public executions rarely had a lasting impact on the population. With the exception of murder, the association between the sentence and the crime committed was hard to establish in people's minds and was soon over and as soon forgotten. Paradoxically, therefore, one needed a constant succession of capital crimes if the death penalty was to retain its effectiveness. Finally, capital punishment did not allow of any degree of proportionality, so that a criminal risking death had no incentive to moderate his or her behaviour in any way in the hope of a lesser sentence. In these cases, the death penalty offered an incitement to crime. Indeed, he believed that executions in general inured people to violence and in some cases even had the effect of glorifying the criminal by turning him or her into a martyr, thereby encouraging rather than deterring crime.

Although this reasoning clearly inspired later utilitarian arguments against the death penalty, such as Bentham's, it rests once again on speculative and possibly mistaken empirical assertions. A convict, for example, would have to break a lot of rocks and sew a good many mail-bags before he began to earn his keep, let alone render a return. As Beccaria's earliest critic – Ferdinando Facchinei – pointed out, it also would be difficult to make much of a deterrent out of hard labour given the harshness of the average peasant's everyday existence. Of course, Beccaria's argument that the death penalty was an uneconomical deterrent had far greater plausibility in the case of the numerous petty offences for which it was still administered at the time, although we have already noted that even here difficulties might arise. However, whilst many of his contemporaries granted this much, even admirers, such as Denis Diderot, felt that capital punishment remained justifiable for murder. Beccaria's clinching argument, therefore, had to lie elsewhere. Namely, that it was the right to punish with death, rather than this or that particular use of it, which failed the test of utility by giving the state a power which appeared contrary to the very purpose of the state and seemed to set it at war with its members, bringing it into disrepute in the process. He contended that to have granted such a power would have been contrary to the utilitarian calculation that provided the basis for the legitimacy of the state. 'For how', he wrote, 'could it come about that the minimum sacrifice of liberty made by everyone included the greatest good of all, life?' (p. 66). Indeed, if, as Christians then claimed, suicide was wrong, the gift of life being a matter of God's will rather than our own, no-one could be said to have a right to kill him or herself which could be surrendered up to others in the first place. The only exception Beccaria entertained was that of an individual, such as a revolutionary leader, whose exile or imprisonment might still constitute a threat to the very existence of the state. However, with the exception of this limiting case, he contended that the state's duty to protect our vital interests could never entail that it put itself at war with us.

Hegel regarded Beccaria's argument as revealing the ultimate absurdity of the contractarian conception of political obligation. For in his view, the state was characterised by precisely this right to call on its citizens to lay down their lives. Other commentators, however, have been less convinced that a prohibition on capital punishment follows so inexorably from the contractarian position. Although Beccaria is often interpreted as having radicalised the Hobbesian account of the social contract, for example, Hobbes himself did not deny the state the right to apply the death penalty in appropriate cases. On the contrary, he believed it was entirely rational that contractors would grant such a right in order to protect themselves from law-breaking by others. He merely contended that the condemned had no duty to obey in such circumstances. Similarly, Kant pointed out in an important criticism of Beccaria's argument that when the contractors cede to the state a right to punish certain crimes by death they cannot be regarded as literally willing their own capital punishment. Rather, they are seeking to create a system of law appropriate to a society which they know will probably contain murderers and other heinous criminals within it. The criminal does not will his or her own punishment, he or she merely opts to commit a punishable deed. From both the Hobbesian and the Kantian perspective, therefore, it is perfectly possible for the contractors to decide that the death penalty might be justified either because of utilitarian considerations as to its general deterrent effect, as in the case of Hobbes, or for retributive reasons concerning its basic justice, such as Kant put forward. At most, Beccaria has simply provided grounds for believing that the utilitarian reasoning of Hobbes's contractors might be flawed. He could only have argued for the absolute injustice of the death penalty had he been prepared to employ some form of natural rights theory which treats all killing as intrinsically wrong.

Beccaria's later writings, most of which were not published during his lifetime, developed the essentially liberal reasoning underlying his theory of punishment. The two fragments reproduced below are the sole remains of a projected work on 'the civilising of nations', although his lectures on public economy fit into the same general vision of human development. Refining his argument, he contended that utility required that the laws operate negatively, to prevent harm, rather than positively, to promote happiness – this latter being best left to individual initiative. As he put it: 'Everything that is publicly useful does not need to be directly commanded, although one should prohibit everything that is harmful. Therefore, all laws that restrict the personal liberty of men have their limit and rule in necessity; and the laws that aim solely at positive utility must not restrict personal liberty' (p. 157). This thesis anticipates in a striking manner the indirect utilitarianism that was to inform Adam Smith's writings. It suggests that had Beccaria lived longer he would have followed Verri in abandoning enlightened despotism as the means of reform and embraced a form of constitutional liberalism.

Beccaria's book made a tremendous impact when it was first published. A comparatively short work, its literary quality and ability to synthesise some of the quintessential themes of the Enlightenment and bring them to bear on a particular issue quickly won it a wide audience. It attracted the praise of the French *philosophes*, who invited him to Paris and encouraged the preparation of a French translation by Morellet. Voltaire recruited Beccaria's work to his own campaign against various abuses perpetrated by the French legal system and prepared a *Commentary* on the text, which was regularly published along with subsequent editions of the Italian's book in French and other languages. The English edition of 1767 brought him to the attention of Bentham, and was subsequently reprinted many times. Catherine the Great even invited him to Russia to help in the preparation of her *ukase* reforming the Russian penal code. Unfortunately, this immediate success proved a mixed blessing in both the short and the long term. Beccaria was unnerved by his sudden fame and curtailed his visit to Paris. Pietro Verri, piqued by the fact that Beccaria rather than he was being credited as the leading light of the Milanese intelligentsia, broke with him. Deprived of Verri's support and that of his circle, Beccaria failed to complete any other major work. Instead, he confined himself to the role of practical reformer in his career as a prominent official in the Austrian administration of Lombardy. These reports reveal a continuity with his early theories. A memorandum of 1792, for example, proposed the abolition of the death penalty and further elaborated the views of his famous book. However, the dissemination of his ideas amongst other intellectuals now largely fell to others and the various distortions that came about in the process went uncorrected. The recovery of his views only began in the 1960s as a result of the scholarly efforts of Franco Venturi and Luigi Firpo. In drawing on their work, this edition aims to enable English readers to come to a fuller appreciation of Beccaria's place within Enlightenment and liberal thought than has hitherto been possible.

Chronology

1738   Born in Milan on 15 March, the eldest son of a reasonably well-to-do aristocratic family.

1746–54   Sent to the Jesuit-run Collegio Farnesiano in Parma, where he receives a 'fanatical' education.

1754–8   Studied Law at the University of Pavia, graduating on 13 September 1758.

1760   Falls in love with Teresa Blasco.

1761   Breaks with family over marriage to Teresa Blasco and forced to live on a small allowance. Encounters the Verris and becomes part of their circle, the so-called Accademia dei pugni. On reading Montesquieu's *Persian Letters* undergoes a 'philosophical conversion'.

1762   Thanks to Pietro Verri, reunited with his family. His daughter, Giulia, is born. Publishes his first work, *Del disordine e de' rimedi delle monete nello Stato di Milano nell'anno 1762*.

1763–4   Between March 1763 and early 1764 works on the manuscript of *Dei delitti e delle pene*, which is finally published in Livorno on 12 April 1764.

1764   Publishes the following articles in *Il caffè*, 'Il Faraone', 'Frammento sugli odori', 'Risposta alla "Rinunzia" ' (an article by Alessandro Verri) and 'Tentativo analitico su i contrabanddi'.

1765   Ferdinando Facchinei publishes his *Notes and Observations on the Book Crimes and Punishments*, to which Pietro and Alessandro Verri reply. Publishes the following articles in *Il caffè*: 'Frammento sullo stile', 'De' fogli periodici' and 'I piaceri dell'immaginazione'.

1766   Morellet's translation of *On Crimes* published. Beccaria and Alessandro Verri visit Paris in October, but Beccaria finds the intellectualising of the *philosophes* uncongenial and, to Pietro Verri's disgust, leaves after a month, causing the two to split. Invited by Catherine the Great to come to Russia to advise her on penal reform. Declines, but the invitation and fame have brought him to attention of Austrian authorities.

1768–9 Appointed to newly created chair of 'cameral sciences' at the Palatine School in Milan, delivering his inaugural lecture in January 1769. Lectures with great success for two years, but his *Elementi di economia pubblica* only published posthumously in 1804.

1770   His *Ricerche intorno alla natura dello stile* published in Milan. Petitions for an administrative post on the Supreme Economic Council of Lombardy.

1771   Appointed to the Council and placed in charge of new legislation on letters of exchange and monetary reforms.

1773   Placed in charge of matters relating to food supplies.

1774–5 First wife dies after a long illness, remarries four months later. New wife gives birth to a son, Giulio, the following year.

1778–94 Rises up administrative ladder, becoming the provincial magistrate for the mint. Thereafter, is employed on a wide range of administrative duties, ranging from the creation of elementary schools, through regulations for trade, industry and agriculture, to a thorough investigation of the penal code, including in 1792 a proposal for abolishing the death penalty.

1794   Dies suddenly on 28 November.

Biographical glossary

D'ALEMBERT, Jean-Baptiste Le Rond (1717–83). French mathematician and philosopher. D'Alembert was the first reviewer of Beccaria's book (in *Gazette Littéraire de l'Europe*, August 1765); and recommended that the book be translated into French. Beccaria's letter to him was occasioned by his favourable comments on *On Crimes* in a letter to Paolo Frisi, 9 July 1765. Among d'Alembert's works to which Beccaria makes reference are: the *Preface* (*Discours Préliminaire*) to the *Encyclopaedia* (*Dictionnaire Encyclopédique*, from 1751), which d'Alembert presented as a paper to the French Academy on the rise, progress and interrelations of the sciences (1754); the *Elements of Philosophy* (*Eléments de Philosophie*, 1759); and *On the Destruction of the Jesuits in France* (*Sur la destruction des Jésuites en France*, 1765).

BACON, Francis, Viscount Verulam (1561–1626). English statesman and essayist, often considered a forerunner or pioneer of empirical methods in science.

BELGIOIOSO, Antonia, Countess della Somaglia (1730–98). Milanese hostess, 'muse' of the Accademia dei pugni.

BIFFI, Conte Giambattista (1736–1807). Cremonese friend of Beccaria, a prominent member of the Accademia dei pugni, credited by Beccaria in a declaration of 1764 with part authorship of *On Crimes*.

BOETIE, Etienne de la (1530–63). See Montaigne, Michel de.

BUFFON, Comte George Louis Le Clerc (1707–88). French Academician, whose *Natural History* (*Histoire Naturelle, générale et particulière* from 1749) greatly popularised the study of nature.

CARDANO, it is uncertain whether Beccaria refers in his Inaugural Lecture to the father, Facio Cardano (1444–1524), a noted Milanese jurist, or to the son, Girolamo Cardano (1501–76), a medical theorist and mathematician who also wrote several books of metaphysical speculation.

CARLI, Gianrinaldo (1720–95); Istrian economist and littérateur, author of several works on monetary reform (*Sulle monete* (1753) and *Osservazioni preventive al Piano delle monete* (1766), put into effect by the Economic Committee set up in Milan in 1765.

CARPZOV, Benedikt (1595–1666). German jurist, a pioneer of Protestant canon law, cited by Beccaria as an instance of inhumane reasoning.

CLARO, Giulio (Julius Clarus 1525–75). Lombard jurist, influential on Carpzov (q.v.). Despite Beccaria's citing him as an apostle of backwardness in judicial affairs, Claro advocated greater leniency than was common in the tradition to which he contributed – a point made by Alesandro Manzoni in his *Column of Infamy* (1823).

CONDILLAC, abbé Etienne Bonnot de (1715–80). French philosopher and empirical psychologist whose *Essai sur l'origine des connaissances humaines* (1746) and *Traité des sensations* (1754) extend John Locke's critique of seventeenth-century rationalism and propose a theory of human motivations on which Beccaria draws freely.

DIDEROT, Denis (1713–84). French man of letters. In his letter to Morellet, Beccaria refers to the *Interpretation of Nature* (*Pensée sur l'interprétation de la nature*, 1754), a fairly systematic exposition of mechanistic atomism, to his dramatic works, prominent among which were *The Natural Son* (*Le fils naturel*, 1757) and *The Family Man* (*Le Père de famille*, 1758), and to the *Encyclopaedia* (*Dictionnaire Encyclopédique*, from 1751), of which Diderot was the founding inspiration.

ELIZAVETA (Elisabeth) Petrovna (1709–62). Tsaritsa of the Russias to whom Beccaria refers in chapter 28 of *On Crimes* because she formally abolished capital punishment for non-military offences in 1754.

FACCHINEI, Ferdinando (1724 or 5–1812). Born at Forli, a Vallombrosian (Benedictine) monk, author of the first substantial criticism of *On Crimes*, the *Notes and Observations* (*Note ed osservazioni sul libro intitolato Dei delitti e delle pene*, Venice, 1765). In some measure, these criticisms were directed at the tendency in Beccaria's political thought to exclude religious considerations; also, in denying (i) the bases of contract-theory; (ii) the primary importance of political freedom; and (iii) the Enlightenment presupposition of egalitarianism, Facchinei can be thought of as being of a similar cast of mind to Edmund Burke. He is credited with having introduced the term 'socialist' (*socialista*) into Italian as a pejorative characterisation of Beccaria's thought. Despite this claim to fame as a defender of the old order, Facchinei began his career writing a *Life of Newton* (1749 or 1751); he continued by contributing to 'progressive' journals on scientific subjects; and he ended with a reputation as a troublemaker within his monastery.

FARINACCI, Prospero (1544–1618). Roman jurist, whose theory of criminal law continued to be dominant in Italy until the end of the eighteenth century.

FIRMIAN, Conte Carlo di (1718–82). Habsburg plenipotentiary in Milan, he was a patron of the Accademia dei pugni and was instrumental in securing Beccaria his professorial chair.

FREDERICK II ('the Great') (1712–86). King of Prussia. Abolished torture to extract confessions in non-military cases on his accession to the throne in 1740; see *On Crimes*, chapter 16.

FRISI, Paolo (1728–84). Milanese mathematician and astronomer; as well as being a Barnabite monk, Frisi made both theoretical contributions to the study of dynamics and practical suggestions in engineering (e.g. on the Brenta canal).

GALILEI, Galileo (1564–1642). Pisan mathematician and astronomer. It is noteworthy that, in his letter to Morellet, Beccaria cites Galileo as a model for his own style in view of the frequency with which he expresses himself as if social and political phenomena are to be conceived of as mechanical and mathematisable (this was an early criticism of Beccaria's style: see Melchior Grimm in *Correspondance Littéraire*, 1 December 1765).

GATTI, Angelo Giuseppe Maria (1730–98). Pisan medical theorist whose work on inoculation, first published in Paris (1763), was translated into French by André Morellet (q.v.).

GENOVESI, Antonio (1712–69). Neapolitan philosopher and political economist, whose *Lezioni di Commercio* (1756–7) proposed a version of mercantilism. Near the end of the *Inaugural Lecture*, Beccaria refers to Genovesi as the 'founder' because, from 1754, he held the first university chair of political economy in Europe.

GIANNONE, Pietro (1676–1748). Neapolitan historian, whose *History of Naples* (1723) attacked the temporal power of the Roman Catholic Church and defended the Habsburg presence in Italy.

HELVÉTIUS, Claude Adrien (1715–71). French man of letters, whose *On Spirit* (*De L'esprit*, 1758) offers a fairly crude version of the egalitarian quasi-utilitarianism also to be found in Beccaria.

HOBBES, Thomas (1588–1679). English philosopher, whose *Leviathan* (1651) was a powerful account of the necessity for men to join together in society so as to avoid the anarchy of the 'state of nature'. Beccaria's argument that the state has no right to execute a citizen has often been interpreted as a radical version of Hobbes's view that a citizen who is to be executed has no duty not to resist.

D'HOLBACH, Baron Paul Heinrich Dietrich (1723–89). Franco-German man of letters, author of many of the articles in the *Encyclopaedia* on chemistry and mineralogy.

HUME, David (1711–76). Scottish historian of England, essayist and philosopher. Hume was a frequent and welcome visitor to the salons of Paris. At the end of his letter to Morellet, Beccaria refers to Hume's kindness to Rousseau (q.v.) in 1765–6: finding himself condemned, expelled or banned from his favourite haunts, Rousseau was fortunate to be invited by Hume to stay first in London and then in a house in Derbyshire; not untypically, Rousseau later found occasion for deplorable behaviour towards Hume.

LAMBERTENGHI, Luigi (1739–1813). Associate of the Accademia dei pugni and contributor to *Il caffè* of a note on the postal service; later politically active in the service of the Napoleonic regime.

LOCKE, John (1632–1704). English philosopher, whose *Essay Concerning Human Understanding* (1690) presented a genetic account of how ideas arise under the stimulus of experience, and the second of whose *Two Treatises of Government* (1690) proposed a version of contract-theory in many ways similar to Beccaria's.

LONGO, Marchese Alfonso (1738–1804). Associate of the Accademia dei pugni and contributor to *Il caffè* of a note on watches; Beccaria's successor in the chair of political economy (1773–89).

MACHIAVELLI, Niccolò (1469–1527). Florentine diplomat and writer, whose political works include *The Prince* (completed 1513), the *Discourses* (completed *c.* 1519) and the *History of Florence* (finished in part 1525).

MARIA THERESA Habsburg (1717–80). Holy Roman Empress, under whose rule (effectively from 1740), the administration of Lombardy was in some measure reformed.

MELON, Jean François (1680–1738). French economist, whose *Essai politique sur le commerce* (1734) was among the first formulations of physiocrat mercantilism.

MONTAIGNE, Michel de, Seigneur d'Eyquem (1533–92). French essayist; in his letter to Morellet, Beccaria appears to be referring to Montaigne's efforts to secure powerful patrons for the posthumous publication of several small volumes of poems and translations by his friend, Etienne de la Boetie (q.v.).

MONTESQUIEU, Baron Charles Louis Secondat de (1689–1755). French political and social thinker. The influence of his largest and most systematic discussion of the nature of society, *The Spirit of the Laws* (*Esprit des Loix*, 1748), is acknowledged by Beccaria in To the Reader and is perceptible throughout *On Crimes* and elsewhere in Beccaria's writings. Beccaria standardly calls Montesquieu 'immortal' (see his 'Introduction', para. 4, and the *Inaugural Lecture*). In the letter to Morellet, Beccaria refers also to Montesquieu's *Persian Letters* (*Lettres Persanes*, 1721).

MONTMORT, Pierre Remond de (1678–1719). French mathematician whose *Essai d'analyse sur les jeux de hazard* (1708) accounts for some of the practical (gambling) principles of probability calculation.

MORELLET, André (1727–1819). French man of letters and first translator of *On Crimes*. Despite being an abbé and a doctor of the Sorbonne, Morellet was associated with the encyclopaedists and wrote several articles for vol. VII of the project (on Fate, Figure, the Son of God, Faith and on the Gomarists). He promised in the letter to which we have translated Beccaria's reply to send books and pamphlets which he had written or translated: two concern the French trade in fabrics; two concern the Inquisition and censorship; and one is the work on inoculation by Gatti (q.v.). In his letter to him, Beccaria refers to an immense and interesting work which Morellet had in hand; this was a dictionary of commerce and economics, which was never completed, although a prospectus was issued in 1769. Morellet gives an account of his first involvement with Beccaria's book in his posthumously published *Mémoires* (1822, vol. I, pp. 163ff.). For discussion of Morellet's influence on the subsequent history of the text of *On Crimes*, see the Note on the texts.

ROUSSEAU, Jean-Jacques (1712–78). Swiss philosopher, whose political and social writings, particularly *The Social Contract* (*Du Contrat Social* 1762) and the *Discourses* (*Discours sur les Sciences et les Arts* (1750), *Discours sur l'origine et fondement de l'inégalité parmi les hommes* (1755) and *Economie Politique* in vol. V of the *Encyclopaedia*) have a clear influence on Beccaria's thought, even when, as in the *Reflections*, Beccaria is critical of Rousseau's vision of the 'state of nature' as idyllic. It is to the novel *Emile* (1762) that Beccaria is referring when he considers education in chapter 45 of *On Crimes*.

SECCHI, Conte Pietro Comneno (1734–1816). Associate of the Accademia dei pugni and frequent contributor to *Il caffe* with articles on a variety of topics (such as tobacco growing, charity and Italian theatre); subsequently a financial administrator in Milan.

SORIA, Giovanni Gualberto (1707–67). The leading philosophy professor at the University of Pisa; he contributed an advertisement to the third edition of *On Crimes* (*Giudizio di celebre professore sopra il libro Dei delitti e delle pene* (Livorno, 1765)).

SULLA, Lucius Cornelius (138–78 B.C.). Roman general and politician who became 'dictator' of Rome (82 B.C.); Beccaria's reference in chapter 26 may be to the centralising reforms which Sulla carried out (e.g. establishing the dominant role of the Senate) and to their short duration after his death; some commentators have seen in this passage a reference to Pietro Verri (q.v.).

TACITUS, Cornelius (*c.* 55–120). Roman historian of, roughly, the first century of the Common Era, and forceful critic of successive emperors in that period; Beccaria's reference to the noxious influence of oracles may be to *Annals* VI 21–2.

ULLOA, Bernardo de (d. 1740). Spanish economist, author of *Restablecimento de las fabricas y comercio espanol* (1740).

UZTARIZ (or Ustariz), Jernimo de (1670–1732). Spanish economist, author of *Theoria y practica de Comercio y Marina* (1724).

VAUBAN, Sebastien Le Prestre de (1633–1707). French soldier and theoretician of siege warfare; Beccaria's reference in the *Inaugural Lecture* is to his proposal, in *Projet d'une Dixième Royale* (1707), that taxation should be levied equally and that the aristocracy should enjoy no exemption.

VERRI, Alessandro (1741–95). Milanese novelist and translator. Although he was co-author with his brother Pietro (q.v.) of the first reply to Facchinei's (q.v.) attack on *On Crimes*, Alessandro ended his days as a conservative.

VERRI, Count Pietro (1728–97). Milanese political writer and philosopher. Pietro Verri was certainly the decisive influence on Beccaria, partly through his setting up of the Accademia dei pugni (1761–2) and his editorship of *Il caffe*, the group's periodical (to which Verri was a frequent contributor), but principally by coaxing Beccaria to write his thoughts out in full. Those few who have doubted the authorship of *On Crimes* have attributed it to Verri; such doubts may have been encouraged by the misunderstanding aroused by Beccaria's remarks in 'To the Reader' which appear to attribute the *Risposta ad uno scritto che s'intitola Note ed osservazioni sul libro Dei delitti e delle pene* to himself rather than to the Verri brothers. Nevertheless, it is clear that the book would not have been written without Verri. Like a number of others at the time, Ferdinando Facchinei (q.v.) appears to have believed that whoever wrote *On Crimes* also wrote *Meditazioni sulla felicità* (1763), called *Discorso sulla felicità* in the second edition (of 1781), which, with his extension of Beccaria's chapter 16 on torture (*Osservazioni sulla tortura*, 1770), is Verri's best-known work. In addition to the composition of various philosophical and political tracts, Verri became practically involved in the reform of Milan's administration and served on the City Council after the French took over in 1796.

VOLTAIRE (pseudonym of François Marie Arouet) (1694–1778). French writer. Voltaire's involvement with *On Crimes* began in 1765 when he was given a copy of the second edition. In September 1766, he issued an anonymous pamphlet purporting to be a commentary on Beccaria's book (*Commentaire sur le livre des délits et des peines*). Because of Voltaire's prominence, it became standard to reprint the book with the *Commentary*.

Note on the texts

On Crimes and Punishments

This text has been surrounded by controversy throughout its history. The first version of the book was written by Beccaria at the suggestion of Pietro Verri between March 1763 and January 1764. Verri then copied out a neat version which introduced stylistic improvements, removed repetitions and changed much of the order of the original. He then sent a fresh copy of this new version of the manuscript to Giuseppe Aubert, his publisher in Livorno, who brought the book out in July. Verri's intimate involvement in the preparation of the manuscript, combined with the fact that his *Meditations on Happiness* had appeared from the same publisher only a few months earlier and that both books were published anonymously, quickly gave rise to the suspicion that they were the work of a single author. Although Verri and Beccaria made clear the separate authorship of the two books at the time, once their relations soured after 1766 Verri was not averse to pointing out his role in the genesis of his former friend's famous work. As a result, a myth grew up that Verri was the true author of the book and that Beccaria had merely contributed a number of disorganised notes resulting from their nightly conversations on the topic. The Verri myth was further fuelled by his authorship, together with his brother Alessandro, of a *Reply to a Piece Entitled: Notes and Observations on the Book On Crimes and Punishments* (1765), which was written as if by the author of *On Crimes* and which Beccaria refers to as his own in the preface 'To the Reader' appended to the fifth edition. Recent analysis of Beccaria's manuscript reveals it to be a far more coherent text than Verri made out, but also confirms that he must have introduced major changes prior to its publication – although his version no longer exists.

In March 1765 Aubert published a third and revised edition of the work, so called because a pirated second edition had been brought out in Florence in 1764 bearing the false place of origin of Monoco. As well as numerous additions, indicated by the author in the printed text, this edition also included for the first time the famous allegorical frontispiece of Justice turning away in horror from the instruments of torture and capital punishment and looking with favour on the symbols of hard labour. A sketch and written description of this design was provided by Beccaria and engraved on the basis of these instructions by Giovanni Lapi. In the meantime, the Abbé Morellet had been producing a French translation of Beccaria's book. Via d'Alembert, Beccaria had sent him a copy of the third edition together with a number of various other additions. However, although Morellet included most of these, he also made a number of substantial changes of his own. Writing in his preface, Morellet maintained that Beccaria's book had the great merit of 'uniting the force of reason to the warmth of emotion'. However, he believed that the latter had occasionally got in the way of the former and led Beccaria 'to lose sight of the most natural order, and prevented him from leading his readers, by the easiest route, to the truths he wished to teach them'. As a result, Morellet took it upon himself to reorder Beccaria's text, altering both the position and even the internal structure of certain chapters and paragraphs. In fact, only four paragraphs remained untouched and in their original place!

By the time the French edition appeared in December 1765, Beccaria was engaged in producing a fifth edition of his book (so-called due to a pirated 'fourth' edition). As with the third, this involved a number of important additions, which Beccaria expressly requested that the publisher should indicate as new in the printed text. Some of this new material had been sent to Morellet, but a number of important new sections, such as the prefatory 'To the Reader', clearly had not been written at that time. Beccaria's reaction to Morellet's edition was ambiguous to say the least. He wrote to him expressing his gratitude and his belief that his reordering was a great improvement. When his fifth edition appeared in March 1766, produced as before by Aubert of Livorno but bearing the false place of publication of Lausanne, and in a later version of Harlem, he had even added a note to the final page observing that 'the French ordering is preferable to that of the author's own'. However, although he had plenty of opportunities to alter his text in conformity to Morellet's, he authorised a reprinting and two further editions of his book which, apart from a few alterations to the frontispiece, left his text completely unchanged. This revision was left to others, when in Venice in 1774 an Italian version of the French edition was produced bearing the false place of origin of London. This so-called 'vulgata' edition, which included only some of the new material Beccaria had prepared for the fifth edition, subsequently became the standard Italian text. It was only in 1958 that Franco Venturi challenged the validity of this decision and argued the case for the version of the fifth 'Harlem' edition. His point of view is now accepted by Beccaria scholars, and the new *Edizione Nazionale* of Beccaria's works reproduces the Venturi text with a few very minor alterations deriving from the discovery of a second printing of the fifth 'Harlem' edition incorporating some amendments to the first employed by Venturi.

The first English translation of Beccaria's book appeared in 1767. Although the translator confessed that he had taken the liberty of 'restoring' a paragraph or two 'to the chapters to which they evidently belong, and from which they must have been accidentally detached', he took issue with the far greater reordering of Morellet. 'I conceive', he wrote, 'he hath assumed a right which belongs not to any translator, and which cannot be justified. His disposition may be more systematical, but certainly the author hath as undoubted a right to the arrangement of his own ideas, as to the ideas themselves; and therefore to destroy that arrangement, is to pervert his meaning, if he had any meaning in his plan, the contrary to which can hardly be supposed.' In so saying, this translator was in good company. Diderot remarked that Morellet had 'killed' Beccaria's book and Melchior Grimm expressed a similar opinion. Unfortunately, later English translators thought otherwise, either because they worked from the French edition or because they were unaware that modern Italian editions had adopted this French ordering. In his preface to the next English translation to be made from the Italian, which appeared in 1880, James Farrer commented that although 'it was translated into English long ago; ... the change in the order of several chapters and paragraphs, which the work underwent before it was clothed in its final dress, is so great, that the new translation and the old one really constitute quite different books'. All subsequent modern English translations seem to have been based on a similar erroneous assumption. This translation, in contrast, follows the text as produced in the *Edizione Nazionale*, vol. I, ed. G. Francioni, Milan, Mediobanca, 1984.

The Letters

(a) To d'Alembert. Written in French, our translation follows the text reproduced in Cesare Beccaria, *Dei delitti e delle pene: con una raccolta di lettere e documenti relativi alla nascità dell'opera e alla sua fortuna nell'Europa del Settecento*, ed. F. Venturi, Turin, Einaudi, 1965, pp. 325–6.

(b) To Morellet. The original letter was in Italian, but only a mutilated copy remains. Our translation follows the text reproduced in Franco Venturi's 1965 Einaudi edition of *Dei delitti e delle pene* (pp. 361–9), which supplements the Italian manuscript with a French translation which was included by Pierre-Louis Roeder in his edition of the Morellet version published in Paris in 1797.

Inaugural Lecture

This lecture was first published by Galeazzi of Milan in 1769. Our translation uses the text reproduced in Sergio Romagnoli's two-volume edition of the *Opere di Cesare Beccaria*, Florence, Sansoni, 1958, I, pp. 365–77, which we have checked against the first edition.

On Luxury

This consists of chapter 5 of Part IV of Beccaria's lectures on public economy, as reproduced in *Illuministi italiani*, ed. Franco Venturi, vol. III, Milan – Naples, Riformatore Lombardi, Piemontese e Toscani, Riccardo Ricciardi Editore, 1958, pp. 189–97. These lectures were published posthumously in 1804 by Pietro Custodi as *Elementi di economia pubblica.*

The Reflections

These consist of two fragments of a projected work on the *Ripulimento delle nazioni.* They were copied out by Giuseppe Biumi, a pupil of Beccaria during his period at the Palatine Schools, in 1771. It is probable that they are based on a book proposal that Beccaria had sent to Aubert in 1768. Our translation derives from the text reproduced in Cesare Beccaria, *Scritti filosofici e letterari,* ed. L. Firpo, G. Francioni and G. Gaspari, Milan, Mediobanca, 1984, pp. 284–304.

Footnotes which appeared in the original texts are indicated by small superior letters; editorial footnotes are numbered.

Bibliographical note

Editions of the texts

Italian editions

As the Note on the texts explains, there has been some controversy over which of the various editions of Beccaria's work best conforms to his final intentions. Cesare Beccaria, *Opere*, ed. Sergio Romagnoli, 2 vols., I Classici Italiani, Florence, Sansoni, 1958, which until recently was the standard edition of his works, largely follows the 1774 'London' edition, as indeed did all subsequent Italian editions. This was the first Italian version to adopt the revised ordering of the chapters made by Beccaria's French translator Morellet, together with the incorporation of almost all the additional material added by Beccaria to the third and fifth editions of his book. The first modern edition to follow the fifth 'Harlem' edition of 1766, the last version of the text overseen by Beccaria personally, was Franco Venturi's, included in *Illuministi italiani*, vol. III, Milan – Naples, Riformatore Lombardi, Piemontesi Toscani, Riccardo Ricciardi Editore, 1958, pp. 27–105. This volume also includes selections from Beccaria's other writings and correspondence. The same text was later used by Venturi for Cesare Beccaria, *Dei delitti e delle pene: con una raccolta di lettere e documenti relativi alla nascita dell'opera e alla sua fortuna nell'Europa del Settecento*, ed. F. Venturi, Turin, Einaudi, 1965. A concordance table indicating the variations between the 'vulgata' edition reproduced by Romagnoli and the Harlem edition of 1766 appears as an appendix on pp. 105–10. Venturi also includes a selection of writings relevant to the origins and the contemporary reception of

Beccaria's book. A new scholarly *Edizione Nazionale* of Beccaria's complete works, under the general editorial control of the late Luigi Firpo, began to appear in 1984. The first volume was *Dei delitti e delle pene*, ed. Gianni Francioni, Milan, Mediobanca, 1984. With one or two minor exceptions resulting from the discovery of a second version of the fifth edition, a few differences over the modernisation of punctuation and the use of capital letters, and the decision to include Beccaria's slightly unreliable indications of the changes he had introduced into his work, this text is essentially the same as the one reproduced by Venturi. This volume also includes a transcription of Beccaria's original manuscript, two detailed essays by the editor and Luigi Firpo on the Italian editions of Beccaria's text, and tables comparing the manuscript with the various editions of the work, including the 'vulgata'. So far the following additional volumes have appeared: vol. II, *Scritti filosofici e letterari*, ed. L. Firpo, G. Francioni and G. Gasperi, Milan, Mediobanca, 1984, and vols VI–VIII containing respectively *Atti di Governo Serie I: 1771–1777*; *Atti di Governo Serie II: 1778–1783* and *Atti di Governo Serie III: 1784–1786*. All three volumes are edited by Rosalba Cannetta, and were published by Mediobanca in Milan in 1987 (vol. VI), 1990 (vol. VII) and 1993 (vol. VIII).

English editions

A first English translation appeared in 1767 under the title *An Essay on Crimes and Punishments Translated from the Italian; With a Commentary attributed to Mons. De Voltaire Translated from the French*, published in London by J. Almon, and by 1775 had gone through four editions. Although the anonymous translator agreed with the critics of Morellet's French edition, English translations of the latter soon came to predominate over those based on the original Italian. The two modern English translations of Beccaria, Jane Grigson's in Alessandro Manzoni, *The Column of Infamy, Prefaced by Cesare Beccaria's Of Crimes and Punishments*, London, Oxford University Press, 1964, pp. 6–96, and Henry Paolucci's *On Crimes and Punishments* in the Library of Liberal Arts series (New York, Bobbs-Merrill, 1963), both follow the 'vulgata' version. Grigson employed the edition published in Milan by Rizzoli in 1950 in the series 'Biblioteca Universale', and Paolucci the Romagnoli text.

Secondary literature

Even in Italian, the secondary literature on Beccaria is surprisingly sparse and in English practically non-existent. Franco Venturi's work dominates Beccaria studies, as it does the study of the Italian Enlightenment more generally. Chapter 9 of his *Settecento riformatore: Da Muratori a Beccaria*, Turin, Einaudi, 1969, together with the introductions to his editions of *Dei delitti e delle pene* noted above, set Beccaria's work in the context of both the *école de Milan* and the European Enlightenment. Some of this material overlaps with two works that have appeared in English: an essay on 'Cesare Beccaria and Legal Reform', in Franco Venturi, *Italy and the Enlightenment*, ed. Stuart Woolf, trans. Susan Corsi, London, Longman, 1972, pp. 154–64, and chapter 4 on the 'Right to Punish' of his *Utopia and Reform in the Enlightenment*, Cambridge, Cambridge University Press, 1971. Stuart Woolf, *A History of Italy 1700–1860: The Social Constraints of Political Change*, London, Methuen, 1979, chapters 4, 5 and 7, and Dino Carpanetto and Giuseppe Ricuperati, *Italy in the Age of Reason 1685–1789*, Harlow, Longman, 1987, chapters 11, 15 and 18 also sketch in the Italian social, political and intellectual background to Beccaria's writings. The European reception of Beccaria's book forms the main theme of the proceedings of an international conference of 1964 published as *Atti del Convegno internazionale su Cesare Beccaria promosso dall'Accademia delle Scienze di Torino nel secondo centenario dell'opera 'Dei delitti e delle pene'*, Turin, Memorie dell'Accademia delle Scienze, Classe di scienze morali, series IV, no. 9, 1966.

More specific studies providing a detailed historical and/or analytical examination of Beccaria's thought are even scarcer. Head and shoulders above the rest are H. L. A. Hart's essay on 'Bentham and Beccaria', first published in the above-mentioned *Atti* and reproduced as chapter 2 of his *Essays on Bentham*, Oxford, Oxford University Press, 1982, together with Giuseppe Zarone, *Etica e politica nell'utilitarismo di Cesare Beccaria*, Naples, Istituto italiano per gli studi storici, 1971. Also of interest are Francesco Corpaci, *Ideologia e politica in Cesare Beccaria*, Milan, Giuffre, 1965, R. Mondolfo, *Cesare Beccaria*, Milan, Nuova Accademia Editrice, 1960 and D. B. Young, 'Cesare Beccaria: Utilitarian or Retributivist?',

Journal of Criminal Justice, 11 (1983), pp. 317–26. Joseph Schumpeter makes some interesting but brief observations about Beccaria as an economist in his *History of Economic Analysis*, Oxford, Oxford University Press, 1954, pp. 179–81. Beccaria's place within the social contract tradition is examined in J. W. Gough, *The Social Contract: A Critical Study of its Development*, 2nd edition, Oxford, Clarendon Press, 1957, pp. 174–5, 183–4. Kant's critique can be found in *Political Writings*, ed. H. Reiss, Cambridge, Cambridge University Press, 1991, pp. 157–8, and those of Hegel in *Elements of the Philosophy of Right*, ed. A. Wood, Cambridge, Cambridge University Press, 1991, para. 100. Three monographic studies in English which deal with the Milanese thinker are Coleman Phillipson, *Three Criminal Law Reformers: Beccaria, Bentham, Romilly*, London, J. M. Dent and Sons, 1923; Marcello T. Maestro, *Voltaire and Beccaria as Reformers of Criminal Law*, New York, Columbia University Press, 1942 and the same author's *Cesare Beccaria and the Origins of Penal Reform*, Philadelphia, Temple University Press, 1973. Unfortunately, they belong to the Great Lives school of intellectual biography.

James Heath, *Eighteenth Century Penal Theory*, Oxford, Oxford University Press, 1963 provides a useful anthology of Enlightenment writing on the subject, including extracts from Beccaria's own work. Part 2 of Michel Foucault's classic study, *Discipline and Punish: The Birth of the Prison*, Harmondsworth, Penguin, 1977, offers a perceptive and provocative analysis of Beccaria's ideas and relates them to the development of penal theory. John Langden, *Torture and the Law of Proof*, Chicago and London, University of Chicago Press, 1976, is a more pedestrian account that suggests ways in which Beccaria's theory could be placed in the context of the evolution of judicial practice.

The two contemporary compromise theories with which Beccaria's theory is compared in the introduction are H. L. A. Hart's in his *Punishment and Responsibility: Essays in the Philosophy of Law*, Oxford, Clarendon Press, 1968, especially chapter 1; and John Rawls, 'Two Concepts of Rules', *Philosophical Review*, 54 (1955), pp. 4–13. C. L. Ten, *Crime, Guilt and Punishment*, Oxford, Clarendon Press, 1987, gives a clear overview of current controversies and presents a compromise theory of his own.

On Crimes and Punishments

In all negociations of difficulty, a man may not look to sow and
reap at once; but must prepare business, and so ripen it by degrees.

Francis Bacon
Essays XLVII ('Of Negociating')

Frontispiece
The allegorical illustration engraved by Giovanni Lapi for the third
edition of 1765. The engraving depicts Justice turning away from
capital punishment in horror and looking benignly on the instruments of socially useful hard labour. Reproduced by permission
of the Syndics of Cambridge University Library.

To the Reader

A few odd remnants of the laws of an ancient conquering race codified twelve hundred years ago by a prince ruling at Constantinople, and since jumbled together with the customs of the Lombards and bundled up in the rambling volumes of obscure academic interpreters – this is what makes up the tradition of opinions that passes for law across a large portion of Europe. It is as deplorable as it is common that an opinion of Carpzov's, an ancient custom noted by Claro, or a mode of punishment suggested with vengeful complacency by Farinacci have become the laws so confidently implemented by those who should tremble at the responsibility of ordering the lives and fortunes of men. These laws, which are the residue of the most barbarous centuries, are examined in this book insofar as they relate to the system of criminal justice. This book presumes to set out their confusions for the benefit of those who are charged with the public welfare in a style designed to ward off the unenlightened and impatient run of men. That sincere search for the truth, that independence of vulgar opinion with which this work is written, are the effects of the benign and enlightened government under which the present author lives. The great monarchs, the human benefactors who rule us, love the truths which are expounded by humble philosophers with an unfanatical zeal directed exclusively against those who, eschewing reason, rely on force or machination. Our current abuses, when their circumstances are fully understood, are a mockery and a reproof of past ages and not of the present day and its legislators.

3

Whoever might wish to do me the honour of criticising this work, then, must begin by understanding its aim, an aim which, far from diminishing legitimate authority, serves to reinforce it, or should do if persuasion is more efficacious than force with men, and if caring and humanity can justify it in everyone's eyes. The ill-digested criticisms which have been published against the present book are founded on confused ideas and oblige me briefly to interrupt my address to enlightened readers and to put a stop once and for all to the errors of timid zeal or the calumnies of piqued envy.

There are three sources from which the principles of morals and politics which guide men are drawn: revelation, natural law and the conventions arrived at by society. Where its ultimate goal is concerned, there is no comparison between the first and the others; but they are all alike in this, that all three conduce to the happiness of this mortal life. To consider the concerns of the last of them does not exclude concern with the first two. On the contrary, it is because these latter, though divine and immutable, have been so corrupted by men's false religions and by arbitrary notions of virtue and vice are twisted in a thousand different ways by impure minds, that it is necessary to examine in isolation from every other matter those things which derive from purely human conventions, both those that are entered into explicitly and those that are tacitly assumed in the interests of the common need and utility, a notion that necessarily commands the assent of every sect and every system of morals. And it will always be a praiseworthy undertaking to compel even the most wayward and incredulous to conform to the principles which drive men to live in society. There are, therefore, three separate classes of virtue and vice: the religious, the natural and the political. These three classes should never come into conflict with each other, although not all the consequences and duties which flow from the one flow from the others. Not everything commanded by revelation is commanded by natural law; nor is everything commanded by natural law commanded by the purely social law. But it is extremely important to treat separately those things which result from this last convention, that is to say from explicit or tacit compacts among men, because it marks the limit of the force which man may legitimately use against man in the absence of a special dispensation from the supreme Being. So, the idea of political virtue can fairly be called mutable, without implying any criticism; the idea of natural virtue would always be clear and manifest were it not obscured by the folly or the passions of men; and the idea of religious virtue is forever one and constant because it is revealed directly by God and is sustained by Him.

It would be mistaken, just because someone is discussing social conventions and their consequences, to attribute to him any opposition to the principles of natural law or revelation, because these are not what he is talking about. It would be equally mistaken for anyone discussing the state of war which obtained before the establishment of society to interpret it in a Hobbesian sense, that is, to deny that there were duties and obligations anterior to the establishment of society, instead of interpreting this state as a fact born of human corruption and the lack of any express sanction. It would also be a mistake to accuse a writer, who is pondering the commandments of the social contract, of denying that there are any duties or obligations prior to the contract itself.

Divine justice and natural justice are both essentially unchanging and constant, since the relation between two objects which remain the same is always the same. But human or political justice, being nothing but a relation between an action and the varying state of society, can vary according to how necessary or useful that action is to society. Nor can human justice be well understood except by one who has analysed the complex and ever-changing relations of civil association. As soon as these essentially distinct principles are confused, all hope of thinking clearly about public affairs is lost. It is for theologians to chart the boundaries of the just and the unjust, insofar as the intrinsic good or evil of an action is concerned; but it is for the student of law and the state to establish the relationship between political justice and injustice, that is to say, between what is socially useful and what is harmful. Neither task can ever prejudice the other, for everyone can see that purely political virtue must give way before the unchanging virtue which flows from God.

I say again that, whoever would favour me with his criticisms, should not begin by attributing to me principles inimical either to virtue or to religion, inasmuch as I have shown that I do not hold such principles. Instead of portraying me as a seditious non-believer, he should try to show me up as a poor logician or a careless political thinker. Nor should he quake at every proposal which upholds the interests of mankind; he should try to convince me either of the uselessness or of the politically harmful effects which might arise from my principles; he should try to show me the benefits of the accepted customs. I have given public notice of my religion and of my loyalty to my sovereign in the reply to the *Notes and Observations*. It would be vain to reply to further writings of that sort. But whoever writes in a tone befitting a decent man and shows a sufficient degree of enlightenment to absolve me from the need to start by proving first principles, of whatever kind, will find in me not so much a man striving to respond, as a peaceable lover of truth.[a]

---

[a] The first additions [i.e. those of the third edition] are enclosed in brackets { } and the second additions [i.e. those of the fifth edition] in brackets {{ }}.

Introduction

For the most part, men leave the care of the most important regulations either to common sense or to the discretion of individuals whose interests are opposed to those most foresighted laws which distribute benefits to all and resist the pressures to concentrate those benefits in the hands of a few, raising those few to the heights of power and happiness, and sinking everyone else in feebleness and poverty. It is, therefore, only after they have experienced thousands of miscarriages in matters essential to life and liberty, and have grown weary of suffering the most extreme ills, that men set themselves to right the evils that beset them and to grasp the most palpable truths which, by virtue of their simplicity, escape the minds of the common run of men who are not used to analysing things, but instead passively take on a whole set of second-hand impressions of them derived more from tradition than from enquiry.

If we open our history books we shall see that the laws, for all that they are or should be contracts amongst free men, have rarely been anything but the tools of the passions of a few men or the offspring of a fleeting and haphazard necessity. They have not been dictated by a cool observer of human nature, who has brought the actions of many men under a single gaze and has evaluated them from the point of view of whether or not they conduce to *the greatest happiness shared among the greater number*. Blessed are those very few nations which have not waited for the slow succession of coincidence and contingencies to bring about some tentative movement towards the good from out of the extremities of evil, but

7

which have sped with good laws through the intervening stages. And that philosopher who had the courage to scatter out among the multitudes from his humble, despised study the first seeds of those beneficial truths that would be so long in bearing fruit, deserves the gratitude of all humanity.

We have discovered the true relations between sovereign and subjects and between nation and nation. Commerce has been stimulated by philosophic truths disseminated by the press, and there is waged among nations a silent war by trade, which is the most humane sort of war and more worthy of reasonable men. Such is the progress we owe to the present enlightened century. But there are very few who have scrutinised and fought against the savagery and the disorderliness of the procedures of criminal justice, a part of legislation which is so prominent and so neglected in almost the whole of Europe. How few have ascended to general principles to expose and root out the errors that have built up over the centuries, so curbing, as far as it is within the power of disseminated truths to do, the all too free rein that has been given to misdirected force, which has, up to now, provided an entrenched and legitimised example of cold-blooded atrocity. And yet, the groans of the weak, sacrificed to cruel indifference and to wealthy idleness, the barbarous tortures that have been elaborated with prodigal and useless severity, to punish crimes unproven or illusory, the horrors of prison, compounded by that cruellest tormentor of the wretched, uncertainty, ought to have shaken into action that rank of magistrates who guide the opinions and minds of men.

The immortal president Montesquieu glossed over this subject. Indivisible truth has set me to follow in the enlightened footsteps of that great man, but the thinking men for whom I write will know how to distinguish my steps from his. I shall be happy if, like him, I can deserve the private thanks of humble and peaceable lovers of reason and if I can arouse that sweet stirring of sympathy with which sensitive souls respond to whoever upholds the interests of humanity.

Chapter 1 The origin of punishment

Laws are the terms under which independent and isolated men come together in society. Wearied by living in an unending state of war and by a freedom rendered useless by the uncertainty of retaining it, they sacrifice a part of that freedom in order to enjoy what remains in security and calm. The sum of these portions of freedom sacrificed to the good of all makes up the sovereignty of the nation, and the sovereign is the legitimate repository and administrator of these freedoms. But it was insufficient to create this repository; it was also necessary to protect it from the private usurpations of each individual, who is always seeking to extract from the repository not only his own due but also the portions which are owing to others. What were wanted were sufficiently tangible motives to prevent the despotic spirit of every man from resubmerging society's laws into the ancient chaos. These tangible motives are the punishments enacted against law-breakers. I say *tangible motives* because experience shows that the common run of men do not accept stable principles of conduct. Nor will they depart from the universal principle of anarchy which we see in the physical as well as in the moral realm, unless they are given motives which impress themselves directly on the senses and which, by dint of repetition, are constantly present in the mind as a counter-balance to the strong impressions of those self-interested passions which are ranged against the universal good. Neither eloquence, nor exhortations, not even the most sublime truths have been enough to hold back for long the passions aroused by the immediate impact made by objects which are close at hand.

9

Chapter 2   The right to punish

Every punishment which is not derived from absolute necessity is tyrannous, says the great Montesquieu, a proposition which may be generalised as follows: every act of authority between one man and another which is not derived from absolute necessity is tyrannous. Here, then, is the foundation of the sovereign's right to punish crimes: the necessity of defending the repository of the public well-being from the usurpations of individuals. The juster the punishments, the more sacred and inviolable is the security and the greater the freedom which the sovereign preserves for his subjects. If we consult the human heart, we find in it the fundamental principles of the sovereign's true right to punish crimes, for it is vain to hope that any lasting advantage will accrue from public morality if it be not founded on ineradicable human sentiments. Any law which differs from them will always meet with a resistance that will overcome it in the end, in the same way that a force, however small, applied continuously, will always overcome a sudden shock applied to a body.

No man has made a gift of part of his freedom with the common good in mind; that kind of fantasy exists only in novels. If it were possible, each one of us would wish that the contracts which bind others did not bind us. Every man makes himself the centre of all the world's affairs.

{The multiplication of the human race, however gradual, greatly exceeded the means that a sterile and untended nature provides for the satisfaction of man's ever-evolving needs, and brought primitive men together. The first unions inescapably gave rise to others to resist them, and so the state of war was translated from individuals to nations.}

Thus it was necessity which compelled men to give up a part of their freedom; and it is therefore certain that none wished to surrender to the public repository more than the smallest possible portion consistent with persuading others to defend him. The sum of these smallest possible portions constitutes the right to punish; everything more than that is no longer justice, but an abuse; it is a matter of fact not of right. Note that the word 'right' is not opposed to the word 'power', but the former is rather a modification of the latter, that is to say, the species which is of the greatest utility to the greatest number. And by 'justice' I mean nothing other than the restraint necessary to hold particular interests together, without which they would collapse into the old state of unsociability. Any punishment that goes beyond the need to preserve this bond is unjust by its very nature. We must be careful not to attach any notion of something real to this word 'justice', such as a physical force or an actual entity. It is simply a way whereby humans conceive of things, a way which influences beyond measure the happiness of all. Nor do I speak here of that justice which flows from God and whose direct bearing is on the punishments and rewards of the after-life.

Chapter 3   Consequences

The first consequence of these principles is that laws alone can decree punishments for crimes, and that this authority resides only with the legislator, who represents the whole of society united by the social contract. No magistrate (who is a member of society) can justly establish of his own accord any punishment for any member of the same society. A punishment which exceeds the limit laid down by law is the just punishment with another punishment superadded. Therefore, a magistrate may not, on any pretext of zeal or concern for the public good whatsoever, increase the punishment laid down by law for a miscreant citizen.

The second consequence is that whilst every individual is bound to society, society is likewise bound to every individual member of it by a pact which, by its very nature, places obligations on both parties. {These obligations, which descend from the palace to the hovel, bind equally the most elevated and the humblest of men, mean nothing other than that it is in the interests of all that the pacts useful to the greatest number be observed. Violation by even one man begins to legitimate anarchy.}[b] The sovereign, as the representative of society, may only frame laws in general terms which are binding on all members. He may not rule on whether an individual has violated the social pact, because that would divide the nation into two parts: one, represented by the sovereign, who

---

[b] {The word 'obligation' is one which is more often met with in ethics than in any other science, and is an abbreviation for a train of reasoning, rather than a mark of an idea. If you search for the idea corresponding to the word 'obligation' you will not find it, but if you reason using it, you will understand and be understood.}

asserts the violation of the contract, and the other, represented by the accused, who denies it. There is, therefore, need of a third party to judge the truth of the matter. Herein lies the need for the magistrate, whose sentences admit of no appeal and consist in simply confirming or denying particular facts.

The third consequence is that, even if it could be shown that the extreme severity of some punishments, even if not directly contrary to the public good and the aim of discouraging crimes, is merely useless, even then, it will be contrary not only to those beneficent virtues which arise from an enlightened reason which prefers to govern happy men than a herd of slaves among whom timorous cruelty is rife, but also be contrary to justice and to the very nature of the social contract.

Chapter 4 The interpretation of the laws

A fourth consequence. Nor can the authority to interpret the laws devolve upon the criminal judges, for the same reason that they are not legislators. The judges have not received the laws from our fore-fathers as if they were a family tradition or a will which leaves its inheritors no duty but that of obedience. Rather, they receive them from the living society or from the sovereign which represents it as the legitimate repository of the current sum of the will of the whole of society. The judges do not receive the laws as obligations of an ancient oath, which is void because it enchains the wills of those not yet born, and iniquitous because it reduces men from a state of society to the state of a herd. Rather, they receive them as the result of a tacit or express oath which the united wills of the subjects have made to the sovereign, as the bonds necessary to curb and control the domestic turbulence of particular interests. Such is the laws' physical and real authority. Who, then, shall be the rightful interpreter of the law? Shall it be the sovereign, that is the repository of the current will of all, or the judge, whose task is merely that of enquiring whether a given man has committed an unlawful act or not?

The judge should construct a perfect syllogism about every criminal case: the major premise should be the general law; the minor, the conformity or otherwise of the action with the law; and the conclusion, freedom or punishment. Whenever the judge is forced, or takes it upon himself, to construct even as few as two syllogisms, then the door is opened to uncertainty.

Nothing is more dangerous than the popular saw that we ought to consult the spirit of the law. This is a bulwark which, once breached, sets loose a flood of opinions. This truth, which seems paradoxical to common minds, which are more struck by a trivial present disorder than by the atrocious but remote consequences which grow out of a false principle's taking root in society, seems self-evident to me. There are mutual connections between all our knowledge and all our ideas; the more complex these connections are, the more ways there are by which we can arrive at or depart from any given idea. Every person has his own point of view, and at different times, every person has a different one. The spirit of the law, therefore, would be the upshot of good or bad logic on the part of the judge and of the state of his digestion, and would depend on the turbulence of his emotions, on the weakness of the aggrieved party, on the judge's relations with the plaintiff and on all those tiny pressures which, to the wavering mind of man, change the appearance of every object. Hence, we see the fate of a citizen changing many times as he progresses through the courts, and the lives of wretches falling victim to fallacious reasoning or the momentary turmoil of the mood of the judge, who takes for the legitimate interpretation of the law the haphazard upshot of this series of confused impulses which affect his mind. It is for this reason that we see the same court punish the same crime differently at different times, because it consults not the constant and fixed voice of the law, but the erring instability of interpretations.

There is no comparison between the irregularities which arise from the rigorous observance of the letter of the law and the irregularities which arise from interpretation. The temporary irregularity occasioned by the former prompts us to make the easy and necessary emendation to the wording of the law which was the cause of the uncertainty; but such an emendation restrains the fatal licence to wrangle, from which arbitrary and sordid litigation arises. When a fixed code of laws, which must be followed to the letter, leaves the judge no role other than that of enquiring into citizens' actions and judging whether they conform or not to the written law, and when the standards of just and unjust, which ought to guide the actions of the ignorant citizen as much as those of the philosopher, are not a matter of debate but of fact, then the subjects are not exposed to the petty tyrannies of the many individuals enforcing the law, tyrannies which are the crueller the smaller the distance between him who inflicts and him who suffers. These tyrannies are more noxious than those of a single person, because the despotism of many individuals is only rectifiable by the despotism of a single person and the cruelty of the despot is proportional, not to his power, but to the obstacles he encounters. In this way, citizens can acquire that sense of security which is just, because it is the reason why men join together in society, and which is useful, because it allows them to evaluate exactly the drawbacks of wrongdoing. It is also the case that they will acquire a spirit of independence, but not the kind that will lead them to shake off the laws or to defy the supreme magistrates, but the kind that will allow them to stand up to those who have dared to sully the name of virtue by describing with that name their weakness in giving in to their self-interested and capricious opinions. Those who have arrogated to themselves the right of passing on to their inferiors the tyrannical blows they have received from their superiors will not like my principles. And I would have much to fear if the spirit of tyranny were compatible with the spirit of reading.

Chapter 5   The obscurity of the laws

If interpretation of the laws is an evil, it is obvious that the obscurity which makes interpretation necessary is another. And it is the greatest of evils if the laws be written in a language which is not understood by the people and which makes them dependent upon a few individuals because they cannot judge for themselves what will become of their freedom or their life and limbs, hindered by a language which turns a solemn and public book into what is almost a private and family affair. What are we to think of mankind, seeing that such is the long-standing practice of the greater part of educated and enlightened Europe? The more people understand the sacred code of the laws and get used to handling it, the fewer will be the crimes, for there is no doubt that ignorance and uncertainty of punishment opens the way to the eloquence of the emotions.

One consequence of the foregoing thoughts is that, without the written word, a society will never arrive at a fixed form of government, in which power derives from all the members and not just from a few, and in which laws which are unalterable except by the general will, are not corrupted as they make their way through the throng of private interests. Experience and reason have taught us that the credibility and reliability of human traditions diminish the further we get from their origins. Without a stable reminder of the social contract, how will the laws withstand the inevitable pressures of time and human emotion?

Thus we see how useful the printing press is, which makes the general public, and not just a few individuals, the repository of the holy laws. And we see how it drives out the shady propensity to cabal and intrigue, which vanishes when confronted with the enlightenment and knowledge that its followers ostensibly despise but really fear. It is for this reason that, in Europe, we see a reduction in the horror of the crimes which afflicted our forefathers, who became by turns tyrants and slaves. Anyone who knows how things were two or three centuries ago and how they are now, can see how, from luxury and ease of life, the most precious virtues have sprung up: humanity, charity and toleration of human error. He will see too what the effects were of so-called ancient simplicity and good faith: humanity groaning under the weight of superstition, greed, the ambition of a few staining with human blood the coffers of gold and the thrones of kings, hidden betrayals, public massacres, every nobleman a tyrant of the common people and ministers of the holy word sullying in blood the hands which daily touch the God of meekness. These are not the doings of the present enlightened century, which some call corrupt.

Chapter 6   The proportion between crimes and punishments

It is in the common interest not only that crimes not be committed, but that they be rarer in proportion to the harm they do to society. Hence the obstacles which repel men from committing crimes ought to be made stronger the more those crimes are against the public good and the more inducements there are for committing them. Hence, there must be a proportion between crimes and punishments.

It is impossible to foresee all the mischiefs which arise from the universal struggle of the human emotions. They multiply at a compound rate with the growth of population and with the criss-crossing of private interests, which cannot be geometrically directed towards the public utility. In political arithmetic, we must substitute the calculus of probabilities for mathematical exactitude. {{Even a cursory look at history shows that disorder grows as the boundaries of empires expand. As patriotic sentiment correspondingly wanes, there is a growth in the motives for crime insofar as each individual has an interest in that very disorder: therefore, the need to stiffen the punishments continually increases.}}

That force which attracts us, like gravity, to our own good can be controlled only by equal and opposite obstacles. The effects of this force are the whole confused gamut of human actions: if these interfere with and obstruct one another, then the punishments, which we may call *political obstacles*, eliminate their evil effects, without destroying the moving cause, which is the very sensibility inalienable from man's nature. And the legislator behaves like the skilled architect, whose task is to counteract the destructive forces of gravity and to exploit those forces that contribute to the strengthening of the building.

Given men's need to come together, and given the compacts which necessarily arise from the very opposition of private interests, we can make out a scale of wrong actions, of which the highest grade consists in those which spell the immediate destruction of society, and the lowest those which involve the smallest possible injustice to its private participants. Between these two extremes are distributed in imperceptible gradations from the highest to the lowest, all the actions which are inimical to the public good and which can be called crimes. If it were possible to measure all the infinite and untoward combinations of human actions geometrically, then there should be a corresponding scale of punishments running from the harshest to the mildest. But it is enough that the wise lawgiver signposts the main stages, without confusing the order and not reserving for the crimes of the highest grade the punishments of the lowest. If there were an exact and universal scale of crimes and punishments, we should have an approximate and common measure of the gradations of tyranny and liberty, and of the basic humanity and evil of the different nations.

Any action which does not fall between the two limits noted above cannot be called a *crime*, nor be punished as such, unless by those who find it in their own interest so to call it. Uncertainty about where these limits lie has produced in nations a morality which is at odds with the law, enactments which are at odds with each other, and a mass of laws which expose the most sterling men to the most severe punishments, but which leave the words *vice* and *virtue* vague and afloat, raising those doubts about one's very existence which lead to the drowsiness and torpor fatal to the body politic. Anyone who reads the laws and histories of nations with a philosophical eye will see the changes which have always occurred over the centuries in the words *vice* and *virtue, good citizen* and *bad*, not as a result of changes in the countries' circumstances and so in the common interest, but as a result of the passions and false beliefs which at various times have motivated the different lawgivers. The reader will see often enough that the passions of one century are the basis of the morals of later centuries, that strong emotions, the offspring of fanaticism and enthusiasm, are weakened and, so to speak, gnawed away by time, which returns all physical and moral phenomena to equilibrium, and they become the common sense of the day and a powerful tool in the hands of the strong and the astute. In this way, the very obscure notions of virtue and honour were born, and they are so obscure because they change with the passage of time which preserves words rather than things, and they change with the rivers and mountains which so often form the boundaries not only of physical but also of moral geography.

If pleasure and pain are the motive forces of all sentient beings, and if the invisible legislator has decreed rewards and punishments as one of the motives that spur men even to the most sublime deeds, then the inappropriate distribution of punishments will give rise to that paradox, as little recognised as it is common, that punishments punish the crimes they have caused. If an equal punishment is laid down for two crimes which damage society unequally, men will not have a stronger deterrent against committing the greater crime if they find it more advantageous to do so.

Chapter 7   Errors in the measuring of punishments

The foregoing considerations give me the right to affirm that the one true measure of criminality is the damage done to the nation and that, therefore, those who believe that the true measure of criminality lies in the malefactor's intention are mistaken. A person's intention is contingent on the impression caused by the objects at the time and the preceding disposition of the mind, and these vary from man to man and in the same man according to the very swift succession of ideas, emotions and circumstances. It would, therefore, be necessary to frame not only a special code of laws for each citizen, but also a new law for each particular crime. Sometimes men do the greatest wrongs to society with the best of intentions; and at other times they do it the greatest service with the worst will.

Others measure the seriousness of crimes more by the rank of the injured party than by their significance for the public good. If this were the true measure of criminality, an irreverence towards the divine Being ought to be more harshly punished than the murder of a monarch, the superiority of His nature off-setting infinitely the difference in the offence.

Lastly, some men have thought that the gravity of the sin plays a role in measuring the degree of criminality of an action. The fallaciousness of this opinion will be obvious to an impartial student of the true relations among men, and between God and man. The former are relations of equality. Necessity alone, from the confrontation of emotions and the opposition of interests, has given rise to the idea of *common utility*, which is the foundation of human justice. The latter involves relations of dependence upon a perfect

22

Being and Creator, Who has retained for Himself alone the right to be at the same time Lawgiver and Judge, for He alone can be both without impropriety. If He has laid down eternal punishments for those who disobey His Omnipotence, what manner of insect will dare to add to divine justice, will seek to avenge the Being Who is sufficient unto Himself, Who cannot be affected with pleasure or pain by anything, and Who, alone among beings, acts without fear of any reaction? The gravity of a sin depends on the inscrutable malice of the heart, which finite beings cannot know without special revelation. How, then, could it be used as a guide for the punishment of crimes? If such a thing were tried, men could punish when God pardons and pardon when God punishes. If men can run counter to the Almighty by blaspheming against Him, then they can do so also by punishing on His behalf.

Chapter 8   The classification of crimes

We have seen what the true measure of crimes is, namely, *harm to society*. This is one of those palpable truths which, though they call for neither quadrants nor telescopes to be discovered, but are within the grasp of the average intelligence, nevertheless have, by a curious conjunction of circumstances, only been firmly recognised by a few thinkers in every nation and in every century. But opinions worthy only of Asiatic despots and emotions robed in authority and power have blotted out, mainly by unfelt pressures but sometimes by violent impressions affecting the timid credulity of men, the simple ideas, which perhaps shaped the first philosophy of those youthful societies, and to which the enlightenment of the present century seems to be leading us back, with that greater conviction that results from a rigorous analysis, from a thousand unhappy experiences and the very obstacles themselves.

It would now seem appropriate to examine and to distinguish all the various sorts of crimes and the ways of punishing them, if it were not for the fact that this would demand immense and tedious detail because of the variations caused by the differing circumstances of differing times and places. But it will be enough to point out the most general principles and the most baneful and common mistakes to correct both those who, from a misguided love of freedom, would wish to introduce anarchy, and those who would like to reduce men's lives to monastic regularity.

Some crimes directly destroy society or its representative. Some undermine the personal security of a citizen by attacking his life, goods or honour. Others still are actions contrary to what each citizen, in view of the public good, is obliged by law to do or not do. The first, which are the greatest crimes, because the most damaging, are those which are called *lèse-majesté* or sedition. Only tyranny and ignorance, which can confuse even the clearest of words and ideas, could apply this term – and a correspondingly severe punishment – to crimes of a different nature, thus making men the victims of a word, as on countless other occasions. Every crime, even a private one, offends against society, but not all aim at its immediate destruction. Like physical actions, moral actions have their own limited sphere of action and, like any other movement in nature, are located differently in time and space; so that only a captious understanding, which is the standard philosophy of slavery, can confuse what eternal truth has separated by immutable relations.

After these, there are the crimes which run counter to the security of individuals. Since this is the main purpose of every legitimate association, the violation of the right to security which each citizen has earned must be assigned one of the heavier punishments contemplated by the laws.

Every citizen ought to believe himself able to do anything which is not against the law without fearing any other consequence than what follows from the action itself. This is the political creed which ought to be received by the people and preached by magistrates scrupulously upholding the law. This is a sacred creed, without which there cannot be a legitimate society; a just recompense for men's sacrifice of that universal power over all things common to all sentient creatures, and limited only by their own strength. This creed liberates and invigorates the spirit and enlightens the mind, making men virtuous with that virtue which knows no fear and not with that pliant prudence which is fitting only to those who have to live a precarious and uncertain existence. Therefore, attacks on citizens' security and freedom are among the greatest crimes, and into this class fall not only the murders and thefts practised by common people, but also those of the nobility and magistrates, whose influence is wider and has a greater effect, destroying the subjects' faith in the ideas of justice and duty, and replacing it with the notion that might is right, which is as dangerous in him who adopts it as it is in him who suffers from it.

Chapter 9   Of honour

There is a noteworthy contradiction between, on the one hand, the civil laws which are the jealous guardians of, above all, the citizen's person and goods, and, on the other, the laws of what is called 'honour', in which pride of place is given to opinion. Long and ingenious disquisitions have been devoted to the term 'honour', without any fixed and stable idea being associated with it. What a sorry state for the human mind to be in, that the most remote and trivial ideas about the revolution of the heavens should be better known than the moral notions which are near to hand and of the greatest importance, forever varying as they are buffeted by the winds of human passions and as they are accepted and disseminated by an easily led ignorance. This apparent paradox vanishes if we consider how objects which are too close to our eyes become blurred. In just this way, the very proximity of our moral ideas makes it easy for the many simple ideas which comprise them to become muddled and for the distinctions necessary to the rigorous investigation of the phenomena of human sensibility to get confused. And the impartial investigator of human affairs will cease to wonder altogether, and may begin to suspect that there may not be any need for such a complex moral apparatus and so many restraints to make men happy and secure.

Honour, then, is one of those complex ideas which is compounded not only of simple ideas, but also of equally complicated ideas, and which includes or excludes its various constituent elements according to the way it presents itself to the mind, retaining only a few common ideas, just as several complex algebraic quantities admit of a common denominator. To find this common denominator in the various ideas which men have created of *honour*, we must look briefly at the formation of societies.

The first laws and the first magistrates arose out of the need to remedy the harms produced by the physical despotism of every individual; this was the end for which society was instituted and this primary end has always been preserved, actually or apparently, at the head of every legal code, including the destructive ones. But the coming together of men and the progress of their understanding gave rise to an infinite variety of actions and mutual needs which always outstripped the laws' provision but fell short of the actual power of each individual. At this stage began the despotism of opinion, which was the only means by which to gain those goods from others and to avoid those evils which the laws were unable to secure. And opinion afflicts both the wise man and the vulgar; it is what puts a higher price on the appearance of virtue than on virtue itself and prompts even a knave to become a missionary providing he finds it is in his interest. Thus men's respect became not merely useful, but necessary, to avoid falling below the common standard. Thus, if the ambitious man seeks it as useful, and the vain man solicits it as evidence of his worth, we can see that the proud man requires it as a necessity. Very many men are ready to stake their very lives on this *honour*. Since it arose only after the formation of society, it could not be placed in the common repository; rather, it represents an instantaneous return to the state of nature and a temporary withdrawal of oneself from the laws which do not sufficiently protect the citizen in such a matter.

Therefore, in extreme political freedom and in extreme subjection all idea of honour disappears or is fully absorbed into other ideas. In the former case, the despotism of the laws makes the search for others' respect useless and, in the latter, the despotism of men, by destroying civil co-existence, reduces them to a precarious and fleeting personality. Honour is thus one of the fundamental principles of monarchies that are mitigated despotisms, functioning in them as revolutions do in despotic states, as a temporary return to the state of nature and as a reminder to the ruler of the ancient equality of men.

Chapter 10   Of duels

Private duels, whose origin lay in the very anarchy of the laws, arose from this need for others' esteem. Duels are alleged to have been unknown in the ancient world, perhaps because the ancients did not foregather in temples, in theatres and with their friends warily forearmed, or perhaps because the duel was a common and ordinary spectacle which enslaved and debased gladiators gave to the public, and free men disdained to be considered and called gladiators because of their private combats.

Attempts to put a stop to this custom by decrees of death against those who engage in duels have been in vain, for it is founded on something which some men fear more than death. Deprived of the esteem of others, the man of honour sees himself doomed to become either a merely solitary being, which would be an insupportable condition for a sociable man, or the butt of insults and slander, whose combined effect would be greater than the danger of punishment.

Why is it that ordinary people for the most part do not duel as noblemen do? It is not just that they are unarmed, but because the need for others' esteem is less common among the humble classes than it is among those who, being exalted, regard each other with greater circumspection and jealousy.

It is not useless to repeat what others have written, which is that the best way to prevent this crime is to punish the aggressor, that is, the person whose action caused the duel, and to absolve him who, through no fault of his own, was compelled to defend what the current laws do not guarantee, his good name, and had to show his fellow citizens that he fears only the laws and not men.

Chapter 11 Public peace

Finally, in the third type of crimes we find particularly those which disturb the public peace and the calm of the citizenry, such as brawls and revels in the public streets which are meant for the conduct of business and traffic. Likewise, there is fanatical demagogy which arouses the volatile emotions of curious crowds, emotions that gain in strength from the mass of the listeners and from dark and inscrutable enthusiasm more than from clear and calm reason, which never influences a large gathering of men.

Among the measures effective in forestalling the dangerous amassing of popular emotions are street-lighting at public expense, the posting of guards in the various districts of the city, sober and moral sermons delivered in the silence and sacred peace of churches protected by public authorities, and homilies in defence of public and private interests in the nation's councils, in parliaments or wherever the majesty of the sovereign power resides. These make up one of the main branches of the care of the magistrate, which the French call *police*. But if the magistrate implements laws which are arbitrary and not set down in a code which is diffused among all the citizens, then the door is open to tyranny, which always hems in political liberty.

I can find no exception to the general truism that every citizen ought to know when he is guilty and when he is innocent. If censors, or other arbitrary magistrates are necessary in some regimes, that necessity arises from the weakness of its constitution and not from the nature of a well-organised government. Uncertainty as to one's fate has sacrificed more victims to a hidden tyranny than public and official cruelty ever has. The latter disgusts men's minds more than it debases them. The true tyrant always begins by usurping men's opinions, and hobbling the courage which can only shine in the clear light of the truth, in the fire of emotion, or in ignorance of danger.

But what shall be the punishments appropriate for these crimes? Is death a really *useful* and *necessary* punishment for the security and good order of society? Are torture and corporal punishment *just* and do they serve the *purpose* for which the laws were set up? What is the best way to prevent crimes? Are the same punishments equally useful at all times? What influence do they exercise over public mores? These questions need to be answered with a mathematical rigour which will cut through the cloud of specious reasoning, seductive eloquence and diffident doubt. I should deem myself satisfied if I had no claim other than that of being the first to present to Italians, rather more clearly than hitherto, those things which other nations have ventured to write and have begun to put into practice; but if, in upholding the rights of men and the invincible truth, I were to contribute to relieving some blighted victim of tyranny or, equally lethal, ignorance, from the spasms and anxieties of death, the blessing and tears of joy of even a single innocent man would console me for the scorn of the multitude.

Chapter 12 The purpose of punishment

It is evident from the simple considerations already set out that the purpose of punishment is not that of tormenting or afflicting any sentient creature, nor of undoing a crime already committed. How can a political body, which as the calm modifier of individual passions should not itself be swayed by passion, harbour this useless cruelty which is the instrument of rage, of fanaticism or of weak tyrants? Can the wailings of a wretch, perhaps, undo what has been done and turn back the clock? The purpose, therefore, is nothing other than to prevent the offender from doing fresh harm to his fellows and to deter others from doing likewise. Therefore, punishments and the means adopted for inflicting them should, consistent with proportionality, be so selected as to make the most efficacious and lasting impression on the minds of men with the least torment to the body of the condemned.

Chapter 13   Of witnesses

It is a matter worth pondering in every good legal code just how the credibility of witnesses and proofs of guilt are to be weighed. Every reasonable man can be a witness, anyone, that is, whose ideas are to some degree consistent and whose sentiments are concurrent with those of other men. {{The true measure of his credibility is nothing but his interest in telling or not telling the truth, from which it follows that it is silly to exclude women on the grounds of their weakness, puerile to treat condemned men, because they are dead in law, as if they are dead in fact, and meaningless to insist on the infamy of the infamous when they have no interest in lying.}} Therefore, credibility should diminish in proportion to the affection, hate or other close relations which obtain between the witness and the accused. More than one witness is needed, because, so long as one party affirms and the other denies, nothing is certain and the right which every man has to be believed innocent preponderates. A witness's credibility noticeably diminishes as the enormity of the crime or the unlikeliness of its circumstances increase, such as in cases of witchcraft and gratuitous cruelty.ᶜ It is more likely that several men should lie in a case of

---

ᶜ {{Among criminal lawyers belief in a witness grows with the horror of the crime. Here is the iron rule which is dictated by the cruellest imbecility: 'In atrocissimis leviores conjecturae sufficiunt, et licet judici jura transgredi.' If we translate this into ordinary language, Europeans shall see one of the myriad maxims, all equally reasonable, to which they are, almost without knowing it, subject: 'In the most horrid crimes, that is, in the least likely, the slightest conjectures are enough, and the judges may go beyond the law.' The absurdities of legal practice are often the products of fear, which is the main spring of human ridiculousness. Our legislators

witchcraft, because it is more probable that illusion, ignorance or virulent hatred should act on several men than that even one man should exercise a power which God has either not given to or has taken back from every created being. It is the same in cases of extreme cruelty since, no man is cruel beyond his interests, his hatred or his fear. Strictly speaking, there is no superfluous feeling in man; it is always in proportion to the effects of the impressions made upon his senses. Likewise, the credibility of a witness can be discounted to some extent if he is a member of some private association whose customs and rules are either little known or different from those of the public at large. Such a man acts not only from his own emotions, but from those of others as well.

Lastly, when the crime is verbal, the credibility of witnesses is virtually nil, since the tone of voice, gestures and everything that leads up to and away from the different ideas which men attach to the same words change and modify what a person says so that it is almost impossible to repeat it in exactly the same way it was first said. Moreover, violent and uncommon actions, which are the real crimes, always leave a trace of themselves in the multitude of circumstances and effects which derive from them; but words remain only in the hearers' memory, which is generally unreliable and often imposed upon. A malicious accusation concerning a man's words is, therefore, far easier than one concerning his actions, since the greater number of circumstances which can be called in evidence about the latter give the accused more ways by which to exonerate himself.

(for such are the jurisconsults who have been authorised by the mere fact of being dead to decide about everything and to be transformed from partial and self-serving writers into judges and lawgivers over men), fearful of condemning an innocent man, weigh down judicial practice with an exuberance of formalities and exceptions such that exact observance of them would enthrone anarchic impunity in the place of justice. When frightened by some few horrid crimes which are hard to prove, however, our legislators believed that they had to overcome the very formalities that they had themselves established, and thus, as much from despotic impatience as from womanish trepidation, they converted grave trials into a kind of game in which luck and guile play the main parts.}}

{Chapter 14   Evidence and forms of judgement

There is a very useful theorem for calculating the certainty of a matter, such as the evidence for a crime. When the pieces of evidence for some matter are interdependent, that is, when the pieces of evidence cannot be tested except against each other, then, the more evidence is adduced, the less credible is the matter in question, because anything which would make the earlier parts fail will make the later parts fail too. {{When all the pieces of evidence for some matter depend equally on a single piece, the number of pieces neither increases nor decreases the probability of the matter, because their joint value as evidence is included in the value of the piece on which they all depend.}} When the pieces of evidence are independent of each other, that is, when the evidence can be tested other than by each other, then, the more evidence is adduced, the more credible is the matter in question, because the falsity of one piece of evidence does not affect the validity of the others.

It may seem odd that I talk of probability in relation to crimes, which have to be certain if they are to call for punishment. But the paradoxicality here will disappear if we see that moral certainty is, strictly speaking, nothing but a probability, though a probability of such a sort as to be called certainty because every reasonable man necessarily assents to it out of force of habit born of the need to act and antecedent to any theorising. Therefore, the certainty which is called for to establish that a man is guilty is the same as that which guides men in the most important enterprises of their lives. {{We may distinguish between perfect and imperfect pieces of evidence for a crime. Those which exclude the possibility that a given man is innocent I call perfect; and those which do not exclude that possibility, imperfect. Of the former, even a single piece is sufficient to obtain a conviction; of the latter, we need as many pieces as are necessary to make up one perfect piece of evidence; that is to say, if, relative to each of the pieces taken alone, it is possible that a man should be innocent, then relative to them jointly, it is impossible that he should be. It may be noted that imperfect evidence from which the accused could exonerate himself becomes perfect if he does not do so adequately. But it is easier to feel the moral certainty of evidence than to define it exactly.}}

For this reason, I think it an admirable arrangement which supplements the main judge with assessors, selected by lot rather than nominated. Because in this case the ignorance which judges by feeling is a safer guide than the erudition which judges by opinion. Where the laws are clear and precise, the judge's task is merely to discover the facts. But, if the search for the evidence of a crime calls for skill and ability, if the presentation of the result calls for clarity and precision, then forming a judgement on the basis of this resulting evidence requires only simple and ordinary good sense, which is less misleading than the learning of a judge who is accustomed to wanting to find criminals and who reduces everything to an artificial system derived from his studies. It would be a happy nation in which the law were not a learned profession!

The law according to which every man should be tried by his peers is a very useful one, because, when a citizen's freedom and fortune are at stake, the sentiments inspired by inequality should be silenced. The sense of his own superiority with which a rich man views the poor, and the indignation with which the inferior views the superior should have no role to play in such judgements. When the crime is an offence against a third party, then half the judges should be the peers of the defendant and half the peers of the plaintiff. In this way, having evened up every private interest which could, even involuntarily, alter the guise under which things are seen, only the laws and the truth shall be heard. It is also in keeping with justice that the accused be allowed, up to a certain point, to dismiss jurors of whom he has doubts; and if this right is allowed to him for a certain time without dispute, then it will seem almost that he is condemning himself.

35

Verdicts and the proof of guilt should be public, so that opinion, which is perhaps the only cement holding society together, can restrain the use of force and the influence of the passions, and so that the people shall say that they are not slaves but are protected, which is a sentiment to inspire courage and as valuable as a tax to a sovereign who knows his true interests. We shall not point out other refinements and provisions which these kinds of institutions call for. If it were necessary to say everything, I should have said nothing.}

Chapter 15   Secret denunciations

Secret denunciations are an obvious abuse, but a time-hallowed one rendered necessary in many nations by the weakness of the constitution. Such a custom makes men dishonest and furtive. Anyone who suspects he sees an informer in his fellow man sees him as an enemy. Men then become accustomed to masking their feelings and hiding them from others, finally getting to the point where they hide them from themselves. Unhappy the men who reach this stage: without clear and fixed principles to guide them, they drift lost and uncertain on the wide sea of opinion, constantly struggling to save themselves from the monsters which threaten them; they live each moment embittered by the uncertainty of the future. Deprived of the lasting pleasures of peace and security, only a few brief moments of pleasure, haphazardly wolfed down in the course of their miserable lives, offer any consolation for their having lived at all. Shall we make of such men the valiant soldiers to defend the nation or the throne? And shall we find among them the upright magistrates who, with free and patriotic eloquence, will support and swell the sovereign's true interests, who will bring to the throne along with the taxes the love and thanksgiving of all classes of men, and who, on the sovereign's behalf, will bestow on the mansion and the hovel alike the peace, security and aspiration to improve one's lot through hard work which is the useful leaven and very life of the state?

Who can defend himself against false accusation when it is guarded by tyranny's strongest shield, *secrecy*? What sort of government can it be in which the ruler suspects every subject of being an enemy, and is forced to preserve the public peace by taking away each individual's peace of mind?

{What reasoning can justify secret denunciations and punishments? Is it public safety, security and the preservation of the regime? But what untoward state of things is it, in which those who hold power and the respect that goes with it, are afraid of every citizen? Is it the protection of the accuser? So, the laws do not defend him sufficiently. And are there to be subjects who are more powerful than the sovereign! Is it the baseness of the informer? In that case, a secret slander is authorised while a public is punished. Is it the nature of the crime? If we call inoffensive or even publicly useful actions crimes, then no amount of secrecy for the denunciations and the judgements will suffice. Can there be crimes, that is, offences against the public, of which it is not in the interest of everyone that it be made a public example, that is, that the condemnation should be public? I respect every government and I am not discussing any one in particular; the state of things is sometimes such that it might appear that the removal of an evil embedded in the system of government spells ruin for the whole; but if it fell to me to establish new laws for some untenanted corner of the universe, I should have the whole of posterity before my eyes and my hand would tremble before I should license such a practice.}

It has been said by Montesquieu that public denunciation is better fitted to republics, where a citizen's first desire ought to be for the public good, than it is to monarchies, where that feeling is very weak as a result of the nature of the regime and where the best arrangement is that of appointed prosecutors who shall arraign those who break the laws in the name of the public at large. But every government, both republican and monarchic, should punish the slanderer as it would the person who is slandered.

Chapter 16   Of torture

The torture of a criminal while his trial is being put together is a cruelty accepted by most nations, whether to compel him to confess a crime, to exploit the contradictions he runs into, to uncover his accomplices, to carry out some mysterious and incomprehensible metaphysical purging of his infamy, {or, lastly, to expose other crimes of which he is guilty but with which he has not been charged}.

No man may be called guilty before the judge has reached his verdict; nor may society withdraw its protection from him until it has been determined that he has broken the terms of the compact by which that protection was extended to him. By what right, then, except that of force, does the judge have the authority to inflict punishment on a citizen while there is doubt about whether he is guilty or innocent? This dilemma is not a novelty: either the crime is certain or it is not; if it is certain, then no other punishment is called for than what is established by law and other torments are superfluous because the criminal's confession is superfluous; if it is not certain, then an innocent man should not be made to suffer, because, in law, such a man's crimes have not been proven. Furthermore, I believe it is a wilful confusion of the proper procedure to require a man to be at once accuser and accused, in such a way that physical suffering comes to be the crucible in which truth is assayed, as if such a test could be carried out in the sufferer's muscles and sinews. This is a sure route for the acquittal of robust ruffians and the conviction of weak innocents. Such are the evil consequences of adopting this spurious test of truth, but a test worthy of a cannibal, that the ancient Romans, for all their barbarity on many other counts, reserved only for their slaves, the victims of a fierce and overrated virtue.

What is the political purpose of punishment? The instilling of terror in other men. But how shall we judge the secret and secluded torture which the tyranny of custom visits on guilty and innocent alike? It is important that no established crime go unpunished; but it is superfluous to discover who committed a crime which is buried in shadows. A misdeed already committed, and for which there can be no redress, need be punished by a political society only when it influences other people by holding out the lure of impunity. If it is true that, from fear or from virtue, more men observe the laws than break them, the risk of torturing an innocent ought to be accounted all the greater, since it is more likely that any given man has observed the laws than that he has flouted them.

Another absurd ground for torture is the purging of infamy, that is, when a man who has been attainted by the law has to confirm his own testimony by the dislocation of his bones. This abuse should not be tolerated in the eighteenth century. It presupposes that pain, which is a sensation, can purge infamy, which is a mere moral relation. Is torture perhaps a crucible and the infamy some impurity? It is not hard to reach back in time to the source of this absurd law, because even the illogicalities which a whole nation adopts always have some connection with its other respected commonplaces. It seems that this practice derives from religious and spiritual ideas, which have had so much influence on the ideas of men in all nations and at all times. An infallible dogma tells us that the stains springing from human weakness, but which have not earned the eternal anger of the great Being, have to be purged by an incomprehensible fire. Now, infamy is a civil stain and, since pain and fire cleanse spiritual and incorporeal stains, why should the spasms of torture not cleanse the civil stain of infamy? I believe that the confession of guilt, which in some courts is a prerequisite for conviction, has a similar origin, for, before the mysterious court of penitence, the confession of sin is an essential part of the sacrament. It is thus that men abuse the clearest illuminations of revealed truth; and, since these are the only enlightenment to be found in times of ignorance, it is to them that credulous mankind will always turn and of them that it will make the most absurd and far-fetched use. But infamy is a sentiment which is subject neither to the law nor to reason, but to common opinion. Torture itself causes real infamy to its victims. Therefore, by this means, infamy is purged by the infliction of infamy.

The third ground for torture concerns that inflicted on suspected criminals who fall into inconsistency while being investigated, as if both the innocent man who goes in fear and the criminal who wishes to cover himself would not be made to fall into contradiction by fear of punishment, the uncertainty of the verdict, the apparel and magnificence of the judge, and by their own ignorance, which is the common lot both of most knaves and of the innocent; as if the inconsistencies into which men normally fall even when they are calm would not burgeon in the agitation of a mind wholly concentrated on saving itself from a pressing danger.

This shameful crucible of the truth is a standing monument to the law of ancient and savage times, when ordeal by fire, by boiling water and the lottery of armed combat were called the *judgements* of God, as if the links in the eternal chain which originates from the breast of the First Mover could be continually disrupted and uncoupled at the behest of frivolous human institutions. The only difference which there might seem to be between torture and ordeal by fire or boiling water is that the result of the former seems to depend on the will of the criminal, and that of the latter on purely physical and external factors; but this difference is only apparent and not real. Telling the truth in the midst of spasms and beatings is as little subject to our will as is preventing without fraud the effects of fire and boiling water. Every act of our will is always proportional to the force of the sensory impression which gives rise to it; and the sensibility of every man is limited. Therefore, the impression made by pain may grow to such an extent that, having filled the whole of the sensory field, it leaves the torture victim no freedom to do anything but choose the quickest route to relieving himself of the immediate pain. Thus the criminal's replies are as necessitated as are the effects of fire and boiling water. And thus the sensitive but guiltless man will admit guilt if he believes that, in that way, he can make the pain stop. All distinctions between the guilty and the innocent disappear as a consequence of the use of the very means which was meant to discover them.

{It would be redundant to make this point twice as clear by citing the numerous cases of innocent men who have confessed their guilt as a result of the convulsions of torture. There is no nation nor age which cannot cite its own cases, but men do not change nor do they think out the consequences of their practices. No man who has pushed his ideas beyond what is necessary for life, has not sometimes headed towards nature, obeying her hidden and indistinct calls; but custom, that tyrant of the mind, repulses and frightens him.}

The result, therefore, of torture depends on a man's predisposition and on calculation, which vary from man to man according to their hardihood and sensibility, so that, with this method, a mathematician would settle problems better than a judge. Given the strength of an innocent man's muscles and the sensitivity of his sinews, one need only find the right level of pain to make him admit his guilt of a given crime.

A guilty man is interrogated in order to know the truth, but if this truth is hard to discover from the bearing, the gestures and the expression of a man at rest, it will be much the harder to discover it from a man in whom every feature, by which men's faces sometimes betray the truth against their will, has been altered by spasms of pain. Every violent action confuses and clouds the tiny differences in things which sometimes serve to distinguish truth from falsehood.

These truths were known to the ancient Roman legislators, who only allowed the torture of slaves, who were denied the status of persons. They are also evident in England, a nation the glory of whose letters, the superiority of whose trade and wealth, and hence power, and whose examples of virtue and courage leave us in no doubt about the goodness of her laws. Torture has been abolished in Sweden and by one of the wisest monarchs of Europe who, bringing philosophy to the throne and legislating as the friend of his subjects, has set them equal and free under the law, which is the only equality and freedom which reasonable men could demand in the present state of things. Martial law does not believe torture necessary for armies, which are made up for the most part of the scum of society whom you might have thought more in need of it than any other class of person. How strange it must seem to anyone who does not take account of how great the tyranny of habit is, that peaceful laws should have to learn a more humane system of justice from souls inured to massacre and blood.

This truth is also felt, albeit indistinctly, by those very people who apparently deny it. No confession made under torture can be valid if it is not given sworn confirmation when it is over; but if the criminal does not confirm his crime, he is tortured afresh. Some learned men and some nations do not allow this vicious circle to be gone round more than three times; other nations and other learned men leave it to the choice of the judge, in such a way that, of two men equally innocent or equally guilty, the hardy and enduring will be acquitted and the feeble and timid will be convicted by virtue of the following strict line of reasoning: *I, the judge, had to find you guilty of such and such a crime; you, hardy fellow, could put up with the pain, so I acquit you; you, feeble fellow, gave in, so I convict you. I know that the confession extorted from you in the midst of your agonies would carry no weight, but I shall torture you afresh if you do not confirm what you have confessed.*

A strange consequence which necessarily follows from the use of torture is that the innocent are put in a worse position than the guilty. For, if both are tortured, the former has everything against him. Either he confesses to the crime and is convicted, or he is acquitted and has suffered an unwarranted punishment. The criminal, in contrast, finds himself in a favourable position, because if he staunchly withstands the torture he must be acquitted and so has commuted a heavier sentence into a lighter one. Therefore, the innocent man cannot but lose and the guilty man may gain.

The law which calls for torture is a law which says: *Men, withstand pain, and if nature has placed in you an inextinguishable self-love, if she has given you an inalienable right to self-defence, I create in you an entirely opposite propensity, which is a heroic self-hatred, and I order you to denounce yourselves, telling the truth even when your muscles are being torn and your bones dislocated.*

{Torture is given to discover if a guilty man has also committed other crimes to those with which he is charged. The underlying reasoning here is as follows: *You are guilty of one crime, therefore you may be of a hundred others; this doubt weighs on me and I want to decide the matter with my test of the truth; the laws torture you because you are guilty, because you may be guilty, or because I want you to be guilty.*}

Finally, torture is applied to a suspect in order to discover his accomplices in crime. But if it has been proven that torture is not a fit means of discovering the truth, how can it be of any use in unmasking the accomplices, which is one of the truths to be discovered? As if a man who accuses himself would not more readily accuse others. And can it be right to torture a man for the crimes of others? Will the accomplices not be discovered by the examination of witnesses, the interrogation of the criminal, the evidence and the *corpus delicti*, in short, by the very means which ought to be used to establish the suspect's guilt? Generally, the accomplices flee as soon as their partner is captured; the uncertainty of their fate condemns them to exile and frees the nation of the danger of further offences, while the punishment of the criminal in custody serves its sole purpose, which is that of discouraging with fear other men from perpetrating a similar crime.

{{Chapter 17   Of the exchequer

There was a time when almost all punishments were pecuniary. Men's crimes were the prince's patrimony. Attacks on the public security were an object of financial gain. Those who were charged with defending the public security had an interest in seeing it broken. The way in which punishment was exacted was by a suit between the exchequer, which dealt these punishments, and the criminal – a civil litigation, more private than public, which gave to the exchequer more rights than those ordained for the public security, and to the criminal more impositions than would be necessary to set an example. The judge, therefore, was more counsel for the exchequer than an impartial seeker after the truth, a tax official rather than a protector and minister of the laws.

But since, in this system, to confess that one was a transgressor was to confess that one was in debt to the exchequer, which was the aim of these criminal proceedings, so it came about (as still obtains, effects lasting long after their causes) that the whole arrangement of the criminal law centred on a confession of guilt put together in such a way as to favour and not to harm the interests of the exchequer. Without such a confession, a criminal convicted on indubitable evidence would receive a lesser punishment than the established one. Without it, he would not undergo torture for other similar crimes which he might have committed. But with it, the judge takes possession of the criminal's body and, with methodical formalities, tears it apart, to draw from it, as from some capital he has earned, all the profit he can. Once the fact of the crime has been proven, confession renders the proof convincing.

45

To make this proof even less suspect, it is extracted by the use of torments and the desperation of pain. At the same time, a calm, impartial confession given out of court, without the bullying fears of a judicial torture, will not be sufficient for a conviction. Enquiries and evidence which throw light on the matter, but which weaken the exchequer's case, are excluded. If criminals were sometimes spared pains, it was not for the sake of their wretchedness and misery, but for fear that this entity, now legendary and inconceivable, might lose its case.

The judge becomes the enemy of the accused, of a man in chains, a prey to squalor, to torture, to the most appalling future; and he does not seek for the truth of the matter, but only for the crime in the prisoner; he sets traps for him and, if they do not succeed, he feels it as a personal failure, an affront to that sense of his own infallibility, which men attribute to themselves in all matters. The judge has in his power the evidence which leads to the arrest. If anyone is to prove himself innocent, he must first be declared to be guilty: this is what is called the *offensive trial*, and the criminal proceedings almost everywhere in the enlightened Europe of the eighteenth century are of this sort. The true trial, the *informative*, which consists in the impartial search for the facts, which is what reason demands, what martial law implements, and what even Asiatic despotism employs in peaceful and unimportant cases, is very little in evidence in European courts. What an involuted maze of strange illogicalities, which no doubt a happier future will find incredible! Only the philosophers of that time will be able to discover through their knowledge of human nature any explanation of how such a system could come about.}}

Chapter 18 Of oaths

There is a contradiction between the laws and the natural sentiments of men in the matter of the oaths which a criminal is required to take so as to make him truthful when he has the greatest interest in being deceitful. As if a man could swear himself into the duty of promoting his own destruction, and religion did not fall silent in most men when their interests were speaking. The experience of every century shows that men have abused religion, that precious gift from Heaven, more than anything. And why should knaves respect religion if the men who are considered wisest have often defiled it? For most men, the motives which religion opposes to the cries of fear and love of life, are too weak because too remote from the senses. The affairs of Heaven are conducted according to laws altogether different from those that govern the affairs of men. Why should the former be confused with the latter? And why should a man be put in the terrible dilemma of being either lost to God or conniving at his own ruin? The law which demands such an oath requires one to be either a bad Christian or a martyr. Oaths slowly become a mere formality, thereby sapping the strength of religious feelings which, in most men, are the sole pledges of virtue. Experience has shown how useless oaths are. Any judge will testify that no oath has ever made a guilty man tell the truth, and so does reason, which rules that every law which runs counter to men's natural feelings is useless and therefore pernicious. Such laws share the fate of dykes which are built straight in the line of a river's flow: they are either flattened and engulfed straight away, or they are eroded and gradually undermined by the eddies which they themselves set up.

47

Chapter 19   Of prompt punishments

The swifter and closer to the crime a punishment is, the juster and more useful it will be. I say juster, because it spares the criminal the useless and fierce torments of uncertainty which grow in proportion to the liveliness of one's imagination and one's sense of one's own impotence. Juster because, loss of freedom being a punishment, a man should suffer it no longer than necessary before being sentenced. Remand in custody, therefore, is the simple safe-keeping of a citizen until he may be judged guilty, and since this custody is intrinsically of the nature of a punishment, it should last the minimum possible time and should be as lacking in severity as can be arranged. The minimum time should be calculated taking into account both the length of time needed for the trial and the right of those who have been held the longest to be tried first. The stringency of the detention ought not to be greater than what is necessary to prevent escape or to save evidence from being covered up. The trial itself ought to be brought to a conclusion in the shortest possible time. What crueller contrast could there be than that between the procrastination of the judge and the anguish of the accused? On the one hand, the callous magistrate thinking of his comforts and pleasures, on the other, the prisoner languishing in tears and dejection. In general, the severity of a punishment and the consequence of crime ought to be as effective as possible on others and as lenient as possible on him who undergoes it, because a society cannot be called legitimate where it is not an unfailing principle that men should be subjected to the fewest possible ills.

I have said that promptness of punishment is more useful because the smaller the lapse of time between the misdeed and the punishment, the stronger and more lasting the association in the human mind between the two ideas *crime* and *punishment*. The former will come to be sensed as the cause and the latter as the necessary, inexorable effect. It is proven that the compounding of ideas is the cement which holds together the fabric of the human intellect, and without it pleasure and pain would be unconnected feelings and of no effect. The further men move away from general ideas and universal principles, that is, the less refined they are, the more they act on immediate associations that are closer to home, ignoring the more remote and complicated ones which are of use only to men strongly impassioned by the object of their desire, the light of whose attention illuminates a single object, leaving everything else in the dark. The more remote and complicated associations are also of use to more sophisticated minds, which have become accustomed to passing many objects in review at one time, and are able to compare many fragmentary feelings with each other, in such a way that the resulting action is less risky and uncertain.

Therefore, the contiguity of crime and punishment is of the highest importance if we want the idea of punishment to be immediately associated in unsophisticated minds with the enticing picture of some lucrative crime. A long delay only serves to separate these two ideas further. Whatever impression the punishment of a crime may make, {it makes less as punishment than as spectacle, and} it will be felt only after the spectators have half-forgotten their horror at the crime in question, which would have served to reinforce their sense of what punishment is.

There is another principle which serves admirably to draw even closer the important connection between a misdeed and its punishment. And that is that the punishment should, as far as possible, fit the nature of the crime. This sort of fit greatly eases the comparison which ought to exist between the incentive to crime and the retribution of punishment, so that the latter removes and redirects the mind to ends other than those which the enticing idea of breaking the law would wish to point it.

Chapter 20 Violent crimes

Some crimes are assaults on persons, others are offences against goods. The former should always be punished with corporal punishment: the rich and the powerful should not be able to put a price on assaults on the weak and the poor; otherwise wealth, which is the reward of industry under the protection of the laws, feeds tyranny. There is no freedom when the laws permit a man in some cases to cease to be a *person* and to become a *thing*: then you will see the efforts of the powerful devoted to discovering from amongst the mass of civil relations those in which the law most favours his interests. The discovery of these is the magic secret which turns citizens into beasts of burden and which, in the hands of the strong, becomes the chain by which the actions of the rash and the weak are shackled. And it is the reason why, in some states which have all the appearance of being free, tyranny is hidden or worms its way unforeseen into a corner neglected by the lawgiver and gathers strength and grows unobserved. Men generally build the most solid bulwarks against open tyranny, but they do not see the tiny insect which gnaws away at them and opens a path for the river's flood that is the more sure for being concealed.

{Chapter 21 The punishment of the nobility

What, then, shall be the punishments fitting for the nobility, whose privileges make up a large part of the laws of nations? This is not the place to consider whether the hereditary distinction between nobility and commoners is useful to a government or necessary in a monarchy, whether it really constitutes a power interposed between and limiting the excesses of the two extremes, or whether it is not rather a class which, a slave to itself and to others, restricts the circulation of credit and hope to a very narrow compass, like those fertile and pleasant oases that stand out in the vast and sandy deserts of Arabia. Nor shall I consider whether, supposing it to be true that inequality is either necessary or useful in society, it is also true that it should subsist between classes rather than between individuals, should be fixed at one part rather than distributed throughout the body politic, or should be perpetual rather than continually destroyed and reborn. I shall confine myself to the punishments suited to this class of person, observing that the punishments ought to be the same for the highest as they are for the lowest of citizens. To be legitimate, every distinction whether of honour or wealth presupposes an antecedent equality based on the laws, which treat every subject as equally subordinate to them. It is to be supposed that the men who gave up their natural despotism have said, *let him who is most industrious have the greatest honour, and let his fame redound on his successors; but he who is more blessed or more honoured should hope for greater things than his fellow men but should not fear less than them the violation of those contracts by which he is raised above them.* It is true that no such decrees

51

issued from an assembly of all humankind, but they exist in the unchanging relations of things. They do not destroy those benefits which allegedly are produced by the nobility but prevent its unfortunate consequences. They buttress the laws, closing off every route by which punishment might be evaded.

To the argument that giving the same punishment to the nobleman and to the commoner is not really fair because of the difference in upbringing and the shame which is brought on an illustrious house, my reply would be that the measure of punishment is not the sensitivity of the criminal, but the harm done to the public, which is all the greater when it is perpetrated by those who are more privileged. The fairness of punishments can only be determined from without, since in reality they have a different effect on every individual, and the family's shame can be alleviated by a public demonstration by the sovereign of benevolence towards the criminal's innocent family. For, as everyone knows, such outward formalities take the place of reason in credulous and admiring people.}

Chapter 22　Theft

Thefts without violence should be punished with fines. Whoever seeks to enrich himself at the expense of others ought to be deprived of his own wealth. But, since this is generally the crime of poverty and desperation, the crime of that unhappy section of men to whom the perhaps 'terrible' and 'unnecessary' right to property has allowed nothing but a bare existence, {and since fines only increase the number of criminals above the original number of crimes, and take bread from the innocent when taking it from the villains,} the most fitting punishment shall be the only sort of slavery which can be called just, namely the temporary enslavement of the labour and person of the criminal to society, so that he may redress his unjust despotism against the social contract by a period of complete personal subjection.

But when violence is added to theft, then the punishment ought to be likewise a mixture of corporal punishment and penal servitude. Other writers before me have shown the disarray which arises from failing to distinguish between the punishments for violent thefts and those by stealth, by trying to set up an absurd equation between a large sum of money and the life of a man; but it is never redundant to repeat what has almost never been put into practice. Once set in motion, political machines continue the longest in one direction and are the slowest to adjust to a new one. These are crimes of different natures, and the mathematical axiom that between different magnitudes there is an infinity of difference holds as true in politics.

Chapter 23 Public disgrace

Personal injuries which damage honour, that is, that proper esteem that a citizen can rightly expect from others, ought to be punished with public disgrace. This disgrace is a sign of public disapproval, which deprives the malefactor of public goodwill, of the nation's confidence, and of that sense almost of brotherhood which society inspires. The law does not stretch to such matters. It is therefore necessary that the disgrace inflicted by the law be the same as that which derives from the nature of things, the same as is dictated by universal morality or the particular morality which arises from particular systems, which are the lawgivers to common opinion in any given nation. If the one differs from the other, then either the laws lose public confidence or ideas of morality and rectitude disappear in spite of speechifyings, which can never overcome the power of examples.

Whoever describes actions which are in themselves matters of indifference as worthy of public disgrace, reduces the opprobrium attaching to actions which are truly disgraceful. The penalties of public disgrace ought not to fall too often nor on too many individuals at a time: in the first case, because when concrete effects are seen too frequently in matters of opinion they weaken the force of opinion itself; and in the second, because to disgrace many people is in effect to disgrace no-one.

{{Corporal and painful punishments should not be meted out for crimes which, being founded on pride, derive glory and nourishment from pain itself. Ridicule and public disgrace are far more appropriate, being punishments which use the pride of the onlookers

to put a brake on the pride of fanatics, and whose constant application can, with slow and patient efforts, bring out the truth. Thus,
the wise lawgiver, by setting force against force and opinions against
opinions, breaks down the admiration and wonder caused in the
popular mind by a false principle, the correctly deduced consequences of which tend to conceal its basic absurdity from the
mass.}}

This is the way to avoid muddling the relations and the invariable
nature of things, which, being unlimited in time and perpetually
operative, breaks down and overturns any limited regulations which
deviate from it. It is not only the arts of taste and pleasure that
have faithful imitation of nature as their universal principle. Politics
itself, when it is true and lasting, is governed by this general rule,
since it is nothing but the art of guiding and concerting the
immutable sentiments of men.

Chapter 24 Parasites

Anyone who disturbs the public peace, who does not obey the laws which are the conditions under which men abide with each other and defend themselves, must be ejected from society – in other words, he must be banished. This is the reason why wise states will not endure, in the midst of effort and industriousness, that sort of political parasitism which is confused by stern moralists with the idleness of wealth accumulated by hard work. This latter is a necessary idleness and useful insofar as society expands and the administration of public affairs contracts. By parasitism I mean that kind of inactivity which contributes neither labour nor wealth to society, which accumulates without ever losing, and which the masses regard with foolish admiration and the wise with scornful compassion for those victims who fall into its clutches and who lacking that drive towards an active life which is given by the necessity of caring for or increasing the requisites of life, let all their energies drift at the mercy of the passions of opinion, which are not the weakest of passions. We cannot call someone a social parasite who enjoys the fruits of his own fore-fathers' virtues or vices and who, in return for his temporary pleas-ures, dispenses bread and a livelihood to the industrious poor, and who wages by means of his wealth the silent war of trade in peacetime, rather than waging with force the uncertain and bloody sort of war. Thus it is not the stern and straitlaced virtue of some guardians of public morals who should decide who are the parasites to be pun-ished, but the laws.

{{It seems as if those who have been accused of a terrible crime and who are very likely, but not certainly, guilty, ought to be banished. To bring this about, however, a law is needed which is as little arbitrary and as exact as possible, and which imposes banishment on him who has posed the nation with the fatal choice either of fearing him or of doing him wrong, but which preserves his sacred right of proving his innocence. The evidence would have to be more persuasive in the case of a citizen than in that of a foreigner, and in the case of a person of good record than in that of a frequent offender.}}

Chapter 25   Banishment and confiscations

But should someone who is banished and excluded forever from
the society of which he was a member be deprived of his possessions? This question can be considered from various points of
view. The loss of one's goods is a greater punishment than that
of banishment; so there ought to be some cases in which, pro-
portionately with the crime, there ought to be partial or total loss
of possessions or none at all. All possessions shall be forfeit when
the banishment laid down by law is such as to sever all the ties
between society and the malefactor. In such a case, the citizen dies
and the man remains, and as far as the body politic is concerned,
this should have the same effect as natural death. It would therefore
seem that the convict's goods should pass to his legitimate heirs
rather than to the prince, since death and banishment are identical
in the eyes of the body politic. But it is not on account of this
subtlety that I dare to oppose the confiscation of goods. If some
writers have upheld the view that confiscations have put a brake
on vendettas and private bullying, they have not observed that a
punishment is just not simply because it produces some good, but
because it is necessary. Even a useful injustice cannot be tolerated
by a lawgiver who wishes to shut out the ever-vigilant tyranny
which entices with temporary advantages and the happiness of a
few notables, whilst scorning the future destruction and tears of
uncounted commoners. Confiscations put a price on the head of
the weak; they make the innocent suffer the punishment of the
guilty; and they force on the innocent the desperate necessity of
committing crimes. What more afflicting sight could there be than

that of a family which is brought into disgrace and destitution by the crimes of its head, when their legally decreed submission to him prevented them from averting his crimes, even if there had been a way of doing so!

Chapter 26   Family feeling

Such lamentable but authorised injustices were sanctioned by the most enlightened men and implemented by the freest republics, as a result of regarding society as a union of families rather than as a union of persons. Say there are one hundred thousand people, divided into twenty thousand families, each comprising five people including the head of the family who represents it: then if the association is regarded as consisting of families, there will be twenty thousand persons and eighty thousand slaves; if it is regarded as consisting of individuals there will be one hundred thousand citizens and no slaves. In the former case, there will be one republic and twenty thousand little monarchies which make it up; in the latter, the republican spirit will be breathed not only in the squares and in public meetings, but also within the home, where much of a man's happiness or misery is to be found. In the first case, since laws and customs are the product of the habitual sentiments of the members of the republic – that is, of the heads of households – the spirit of monarchism will gradually infiltrate the republic itself and the effects of this change will be curbed only by the conflict of individual interests, and not by an atmosphere of freedom and equality. Family feeling is a feeling for details and is limited to small matters. The spirit which regulates republics involves mastery of general principles, identifies the essential facts and reduces them to the main classes which are important for the good of the greatest number. In the republic of families, children remain under the power of the head so long as he lives, and have to wait until he dies to live under the sole jurisdiction of the laws. Habituated to bowing and scraping and going in fear at an age when they are freshest and most lively, when their feelings are least affected by that fear of experience which goes by the name of moderation, how will they overcome the obstacles which vice always places in the way of virtue in their sluggish and decaying years, when men tend to oppose any dramatic changes, among other reasons because they despair of ever seeing the results?

When a republic is made up of persons, subordination within the family is not a matter of command but of contract; and when the children, having outgrown the natural dependence resulting from their weakness and need for education and protection, become free members of the city, they submit to the head of the family in order to share in its advantages, just as free men do in society at large. In the case of a republic made up of families, the sons, who constitute the largest and most productive part of the community, are at their father's disposal. In a republic made up of persons, there is no obligatory bond other than the sacred and inviolable call to give all necessary mutual aid and the duty to show gratitude for kindnesses received – a bond undermined less by the malignancy of the human heart than it is by being misguidedly imposed by the laws.

Such conflicts between the laws of the family and the basic laws of the republic are a rich source of other conflicts between domestic and public morality, and thus produce a perpetual strife within the soul of each man. The first of these laws inspires submissiveness and fear, the second courage and free-spiritedness; the first teaches one to limit beneficence to a small number of people whom one has not oneself chosen, the second to extend it to all classes of men; the former demands continual self-sacrifice to a false idol going by the name of the *good of the family*, which is frequently not the good of any of its members, while the latter teaches one to seek one's own interest without breaking the laws or excites the passionate feeling which spurs one to sacrifice oneself for the nation. Such conflicts lead men to spurn the pursuit of virtue, which they find incoherent and confused, and as remote as all blurred objects, both physical and moral, appear. How often, in thinking over his past actions, is a man astonished to find that he has acted wrongly!

As society grows, each individual becomes a smaller fraction of the whole, and the republican sentiment diminishes at the same rate unless the laws take care to reinforce it. Like the human body, societies have their circumscribed limits and, if they grow beyond them, their economy will be upset. It seems as if the size of a state should be in inverse proportion to the sensibility of its members, otherwise, if both were to grow at the same rate, even good laws would find that the very good which they have produced will be an obstacle to the prevention of crimes. Too large a republic will not save itself from despotism except by subdividing itself and uniting into so many federated republics. But how is this end to be achieved? By a despotic dictator with the courage of Sulla, and as much flair for building as he had for destroying. If such a man is ambitious, the renown of future centuries awaits him; if he is a philosopher, the blessing of his fellow citizens will requite him for the loss of power, if he has not already become indifferent to their ingratitude. As the feelings which attach us to our nation weaken, so our feelings for the things close to hand are strengthened; thus under the harshest despotisms friendships are at their strongest, and the always modest virtues of the family are the most common or rather the only ones. From this fact anyone can see how limited the vision of most lawgivers has been.

Chapter 27 Lenience in punishing

But my thoughts have carried me away from my topic, which I must now waste no time in returning to. One of the most effective brakes on crime is not the harshness of its punishment, but the unerringness of punishment. This calls for vigilance in the magistrates, and that kind of unswerving judicial severity which, to be useful to the cause of virtue, must be accompanied by a lenient code of laws. The certainty of even a mild punishment will make a bigger impression than the fear of a more awful one which is united to a hope of not being punished at all. For, even the smallest harms, when they are certain, always frighten human souls, whereas hope, that heavenly gift which often displaces every other sentiment, holds at bay the idea of larger harms, especially when it is reinforced by frequent examples of the impunity accorded by weak and corrupt judges. The harsher the punishment and the worse the evil he faces, the more anxious the criminal is to avoid it, and it makes him commit other crimes to escape the punishment of the first. The times and places in which the penalties have been fiercest have been those of the bloodiest and most inhuman actions. Because the same brutal spirit which guided the hand of the lawgiver, also moved the parricide's and the assassin's. He decreed iron laws from the throne for the savage souls of slaves, who duly obeyed them; and in secluded darkness he urged men to murder tyrants only to create new ones.

As punishments become harsher, human souls which, like fluids, find their level from their surroundings, become hardened and the ever lively power of the emotions brings it about that, after a hundred years of cruel tortures, the wheel only causes as much fear as prison previously did. If a punishment is to serve its purpose, it is enough that the harm of punishment should outweigh the good which the criminal can derive from the crime, and into the calculation of this balance, we must add the unerringness of the punishment and the loss of the good produced by the crime. Anything more than this is superfluous and, therefore, tyrannous. Men are guided by the repeated action on them of the harms they know and not by those they do not. Imagine two states, in which the scales of punishment are proportionate to the crimes and that in one the worst punishment is perpetual slavery, and that in the other it is breaking on the wheel. I maintain that there would be as much fear of the worst punishment in the first as in the second; and if there were cause to introduce in the first the worst punishments of the second, the same cause would produce an increase in the punishments of the second, which would gradually move from the wheel via slower and more elaborate torments to reach the ultimate refinements of that science which tyrants know all too well.

Two other disastrous consequences contrary to the very purpose of preventing crime follow from having harsh punishments. One is that it is not easy to sustain the necessary proportion between crime and punishment because, despite all the efforts of cruelty to devise all manner of punishments, they still cannot go beyond the limits of endurance of the human organism and feeling. Once this point has been reached, no correspondingly greater punishments necessary to prevent the more damaging and atrocious crimes can be found. The other consequence is that the harshness of punishments gives rise to impunity. Men's capacity for good or evil is confined within certain bounds, and a spectacle which is too awful for humanity cannot be more than a temporary upset, and can never become a fixed system of the sort proper to the law. If the laws are truly cruel, they must either be changed or they will occasion a fatal impunity.

What reader of history does not shudder with horror at the barbaric and useless tortures that so-called wise men have cold-bloodedly invented and put into operation? Who can fail to feel himself shaken to the core by the sight of thousands of wretches whom poverty, either willed or tolerated by the laws, which have always favoured the few and abused the masses, has dragged back to the primitive state of nature, and either accused of impossible crimes invented out of a cringing ignorance or found guilty of nothing but being faithful to their own principles, and who are then torn apart with premeditated pomp and slow tortures by men with the same faculties and emotions, becoming the entertainment of a fanatical mob?

Chapter 28   The death penalty

I am prompted by this futile excess of punishments, which have never made men better, to enquire whether the death penalty is really useful and just in a well-organised state. By what right can men presume to slaughter their fellows? Certainly not that right which is the foundation of sovereignty and the laws. For these are nothing but the sum of the smallest portions of each man's own freedom; they represent the general will which is the aggregate of the individual wills. Who has ever willingly given up to others the authority to kill him? How on earth can the minimum sacrifice of each individual's freedom involve handing over the greatest of all goods, life itself? And even if that were so, how can it be reconciled with the other principle which denies that a man is free to commit suicide, which he must be, if he is able to transfer that right to others or to society as a whole?

Thus, the death penalty is not a matter of *right*, as I have just shown, but is an act of war on the part of society against the citizen that comes about when it is deemed necessary or useful to destroy his existence. But if I can go on to prove that such a death is neither necessary nor useful, I shall have won the cause of humanity.

There are only two grounds on which the death of a citizen might be held to be necessary. First, when it is evident that even if deprived of his freedom, he retains such connections and such power as to endanger the security of the nation, when, that is, his existence may threaten a dangerous revolution in the established form of government. The death of a citizen becomes necessary, therefore, when the nation stands to gain or lose its freedom, or in periods of anarchy, when disorder replaces the laws. But when the rule of law calmly prevails, under a form of government behind which the people are united, which is secured from without and from within, both by its strength and, perhaps more efficacious than force itself, by public opinion, in which the control of power is in the hands of the true sovereign, in which wealth buys pleasures and not influence, then I do not see any need to destroy a citizen, unless his death is the true and only brake to prevent others from committing crimes, which is the second ground for thinking the death penalty just and necessary.

Although men, who always suspect the voice of reason and respect that of authority, have not been persuaded by the experience of centuries, during which the ultimate penalty has never dissuaded men from offending against society, nor by the example of the citizens of Rome, nor by the twenty years of the reign of the Empress Elizabeth of Muscovy, in which she set the leaders of all peoples an outstanding precedent, worth at least as much as many victories bought with the blood of her motherland's sons, it will suffice to consult human nature to be convinced of the truth of my claim.

It is not the intensity, but the extent of a punishment which makes the greatest impression on the human soul. For our sensibility is more easily and lastingly moved by minute but repeated impressions than by a sharp but fleeting shock. Habit has universal power over every sentient creature. Just as a man speaks and walks and goes about his business with its help, so moral ideas are only impressed on his mind by lasting and repeated blows. It is not the terrible but fleeting sight of a felon's death which is the most powerful brake on crime, but the long-drawn-out example of a man deprived of freedom, who having become a beast of burden, repays the society which he has offended with his labour. Much more potent than the idea of death, which men always regard as vague and distant, is the efficacious because often repeated reflection that *I too shall be reduced to so dreary and so pitiable a state if I commit similar crimes.*

For all its vividness, the impression made by the death penalty cannot compensate for the forgetfulness of men, even in the most important matters, which is natural and speeded by the passions.

As a general rule, violent passions take hold of men but not for long; thus they are suited to producing those revolutions which make normal men into Persians or Spartans; whereas the impressions made in a free and peaceful state should be frequent rather than strong.

For most people, the death penalty becomes a spectacle and for the few an object of compassion mixed with scorn. Both these feelings occupy the minds of the spectators more than the salutary fear which the law claims to inspire. But with moderate and continuous punishments it is this last which is the dominant feeling, because it is the only one. The limit which the lawgiver should set to the harshness of punishments seems to depend on when the feeling of compassion at a punishment, meant more for the spectators than for the convict, begins to dominate every other in their souls.

{If a punishment is to be just, it must be pitched at just that level of intensity which suffices to deter men from crime. Now there is no-one who, after considering the matter, could choose the total and permanent loss of his own freedom, however profitable the crime might be. Therefore, permanent penal servitude in place of the death penalty would be enough to deter even the most resolute soul: indeed, I would say that it is more likely to. Very many people look on death with a calm and steadfast gaze, some from fanaticism, some from vanity, a sentiment that almost always accompanies a man to the grave and beyond, and some from a last desperate effort either to live no more or to escape from poverty. However, neither fanaticism nor vanity survives in manacles and chains, under the rod and the yoke or in an iron cage; and the ills of the desperate man are not over, but are just beginning. Our spirit withstands violence and extreme but fleeting pains better than time and endless fatigue. For it can, so to speak, condense itself to repel the former, but its tenacious elasticity is insufficient to resist the latter.

With the death penalty, every lesson which is given to the nation requires a new crime; with permanent penal servitude, a single crime gives very many lasting lessons. And, if it is important that men often see the power of the law, executions ought not to be too infrequent: they therefore require there to be frequent crimes; so that, if this punishment is to be effective, it is necessary that it not make the impression that it should make. That is, it must be both useful and useless at the same time. If it be said that permanent penal servitude is as grievous as death, and therefore as cruel, I reply that, if we add up all the unhappy moments of slavery, perhaps it is even more so, but the latter are spread out over an entire life, whereas the former exerts its force only at a single moment. And this is an advantage of penal servitude, because it frightens those who see it more than those who undergo it. For the former thinks about the sum of unhappy moments, whereas the latter is distracted from present unhappiness by the prospect of future pain. All harms are magnified in the imagination, and the sufferer finds resources and consolations unknown and unsuspected by the spectators, who put their own sensibility in the place of the hardened soul of the wretch.}

A thief or murderer who has nothing to weigh against breaking the law except the gallows or the wheel reasons pretty much along the following lines. (I know that self-analysis is a skill which we acquire with education; but just because a thief would not express his principles well, it does not mean that he lacks them.) *What are these laws which I have to obey, which leave such a gulf between me and the rich man? He denies me the penny I beg of him, brushing me off with the demand that I should work, something he knows nothing about. Who made these laws? Rich and powerful men, who have never condescended to visit the filthy hovels of the poor, who have never broken mouldy bread among the innocent cries of starving children and a wife's tears. Let us break these ties, which are pernicious to most people and only useful to a few and idle tyrants; let us attack injustice at its source. I shall return to my natural state of independence; for a while I shall live free and happy on the fruits of my courage and industry; perhaps the day for suffering and repentance will come, but it will be brief, and I shall have one day of pain for many years of freedom and pleasure. King of a small band of men, I shall put to rights the iniquities of fortune, and I shall see these tyrants blanch and cower at one whom they considered, with insulting ostentation, lower than their horses and dogs.* Then, religion comes into the mind of the ruffian, who makes ill-use of everything, and, offering an easy repentance and near-certainty of eternal bliss, considerably diminishes for him the horror of the last tragedy.

But a man who sees ahead of him many years, or even the remainder of his life, passed in slavery and suffering before the eyes of his fellow citizens, with whom he currently lives freely and sociably, the slave of those laws by which he was protected, will make a salutary calculation, balancing all of that against the uncertainty of the outcome of his crimes, and the shortness of the time in which he could enjoy their fruit. The continued example of those whom he now sees as the victims of their own lack of foresight, will make a stronger impression on him than would a spectacle which hardens more than it reforms him.

The death penalty is not useful because of the example of savagery it gives to men. If our passions or the necessity of war have taught us how to spill human blood, laws, which exercise a moderating influence on human conduct, ought not to add to that cruel example, which is all the more grievous the more a legal killing is carried out with care and pomp. It seems absurd to me that the laws, which are the expression of the public will, and which hate and punish murder, should themselves commit one, and that to deter citizens from murder, they should decree a public murder. What are the true and most useful laws? Those contracts and terms that everyone would want to obey and to propose so long as the voice of private interest, which is always listened to, is silent or in agreement with the public interest. What are everyone's feelings about the death penalty? We can read them in the indignation and contempt everyone feels for the hangman, who is after all the innocent executor of the public will, a good citizen who contributes to the public good, as necessary an instrument of public security within the state as the valiant soldier is without. What, then, is the root of this conflict? And why is this feeling ineradicable in men, in spite of reason? It is because, deep within their souls, that part which still retains elements of their primitive nature, men have always believed that no-one and nothing should hold the power of life and death over them but necessity, which rules the universe with its iron rod.

What are men to think when they see the wise magistrates and the solemn ministers of justice order a convict to be dragged to his death with slow ceremony, or when a judge, with cold equanimity and even with a secret complacency in his own authority, can pass by a wretch convulsed in his last agonies, awaiting the *coup de grâce*, to savour the comforts and pleasures of life? *Ah!*, they will say, *these laws are nothing but pretexts for power and for the calculated and cruel formalities of justice; they are nothing but a conven-*

tional language for killing us all the more surely, like the preselected victims of a sacrifice to the insatiable god of despotism. Murder, which we have preached to us as a terrible crime, we see instituted without disgust and without anger. Let us profit from this example. From the descriptions we have been given of it, violent death seemed to be a terrible thing, but we see it to be the work of a minute. How much the less it will be for him who, unaware of its coming, is spared almost everything about it which is most painful! This is the horrific casuistry which, if not clearly, at least confusedly, leads men – in whom, as we have seen, the abuse of religion can be more powerful than religion itself – to commit crimes.

If it is objected that almost all times and almost all places have used the death penalty for some crimes, I reply that the objection collapses before the truth, against which there is no appeal, that the history of mankind gives the impression of a vast sea of errors, among which a few confused truths float at great distances from each other. Human sacrifices were common to almost all nations; but who would dare to justify them? That only a few societies have given up inflicting the death penalty, and only for a brief time, is actually favourable to my argument, because it is what one would expect to be the career of the great truths, which last but a flash compared with the long and dark night which engulfs mankind. The happy time has not yet begun in which the truth, like error hitherto, is the property of the many. Up until now, the only truths which have been excepted from this universal rule have been those which the infinite Wisdom wished to distinguish from the others by revealing them.

The voice of a philosopher is too weak against the uproar and the shouting of those who are guided by blind habit. But what I say will find an echo in the hearts of the few wise men who are scattered across the face of the earth. And if truth, in the face of the thousand obstacles which, against his wishes, keep it far from the monarch, should arrive at his throne, let him know that it arrives with the secret support of all men, and let him know that its glory will silence the blood-stained reputation of conquerors and that the justice of future ages will award him peaceful trophies above those of the Tituses, the Antonines and the Trajans.

How happy humanity would be if laws were being decreed for the first time, now that we see seated on the thrones of Europe benevolent monarchs, inspirers of the virtues of peace, of the sciences, of the arts, fathers of their peoples, crowned citizens. Their increased power serves the happiness of their subjects because it removes that crueller, because more capricious intermediary despotism, which choked the always sincere desires of the people which are always beneficial when they may approach the throne! If they leave the ancient laws in place, I say, it is because of the endless difficulty of removing the venerated and centuries-old rust. That is a reason for enlightened citizens to wish all the more fervently for their authority to continue to increase.

Chapter 29   Of detention awaiting trial

A mistake no less common for being against the purpose of society, namely a sense of one's own security, is to allow a judge, who is the executor of the law, to be free to detain citizens, to deprive an enemy of his freedom on the slightest pretexts, and to let a friend avoid punishment in spite of the strongest evidence of guilt. Unlike every other sort of punishment, detention necessarily precedes conviction for a crime. But this peculiar characteristic does not set aside that other essential principle, which is that the law alone should determine the cases in which a man deserves to be punished. The law, therefore, should indicate what kinds of criminal evidence justify the detention of the accused, and expose him to investigation and imprisonment. Public repute, flight, confession, denunciation by an accomplice, threats, and continued hostility to the crime's victim, the circumstances of the crime, and similar evidence are sufficient proofs to imprison a citizen. But such proofs have to be established by law and not by judges, whose rulings are always contrary to public safety when they are not particular applications of general rules laid down in statute. The laws can be satisfied with ever weaker evidence for imprisonment as the punishments become more humane, as prisons become less appalling and infamous places, as compassion and humanity enter their iron gates and take control of the inflexible and hardened ministers of justice.

A man accused of a crime, remanded in custody and acquitted should bear no mark of shame. How many Romans, who were accused of the most serious crimes and then found innocent, were revered by the people and honoured by the magistracy! But why is the fate of an innocent man so different today? Because it seems that, in our current criminal system, the idea of force and power predominates in the popular mind over the idea of justice; because the accused and the convicted are thrown together into the same dungeon; because prison is more a punishment than a place of custody of the accused, {{and because the force that upholds the laws internally is separated from the force that defends the throne and the nation, when they ought to be united. If they were so united, the former would be joined to the judicial arm by their common reliance on the laws, although it would not be dependent on the latter's direct authority. And the glory which accompanies the pomp and pride of a military unit would draw off the ill-repute which, like all vulgar feelings, attaches to the manner rather than to the thing; and this is shown by military prisons' not being as shameful in the common mind as civil prisons.}} The barbaric notions and fierce ideas of our ancestral northern huntsmen still remain in the popular mind, in our customs and in our laws, which are always a hundred years behind a given nation's stage of goodness and enlightenment.

It has been maintained by some people that, wherever a crime or illegal action is committed, it can be punished; as if the status of being a subject were indelible, like that of a slave. Or even worse, as if a person could be the subject of one government and live under another, and as if his actions could, without contradiction, fall under two sovereigns and two, often contradictory, codes of law. Some believe likewise, on the abstract grounds that one who offends against mankind deserves universal condemnation and to have all mankind as his enemy, that an evil act committed at Constantinople, for instance, can be punished in Paris. As if judges were the upholders of human sensibilities, rather than of the contracts which bind men together. The place of punishment is the place of the crime, because it is there and nowhere else that men must settle accounts with an individual to prevent an affront to the public. A villain, provided he has not broken the terms of a society of which he is not a member, may be feared and so exiled and excluded by the greater power of the society, but he may not be punished by the processes of law which enforce contracts but do not pursue the intrinsic evil of actions.

Those guilty of lesser crimes are often punished either in the dark of the prison-house or by being deported as an example to a distant, and so almost useless, slavery in countries where they have not offended. Since men do not suddenly decide to commit great crimes, most people will regard the public punishment of a serious crime as nothing to do with them and as something that could never happen to them. But the public punishment of lesser crimes, which seem to be closer to home, would make more of an impression, and in deterring men from these would deter them all the more from the others. Punishments should be proportional among themselves to crimes, not only in their severity but also in the manner in which they are inflicted. Some would excuse the punishment of a petty crime if the offended party forgives the criminal, an act of beneficence and humanity but contrary to the public good. As if the pardon of a private citizen could remove the necessity of setting an example in the same way that he can forgo damages for the offence. The right to have someone punished does not belong to any individual; it is the right of all the citizens and of the sovereign. The individual can give up his part of this right, but he cannot cancel that of others.

Chapter 30   Trials and prescriptions

Once the evidence has been collected and the crime established, it is necessary to allow the accused time and the means to clear himself. But the time should be brief so as not to compromise the promptness of punishment, which we have seen to be one of the main brakes on crime. Some have opposed such brevity out of a misguided love of humanity, but all doubts will vanish once it is recognised that it is the defects in the laws that increase the dangers to the innocent.

But the laws ought to establish a certain amount of time for preparing both the defence and the prosecution, and the judge would become a lawmaker if it fell to him to decide how much time was to be set aside for trying a given crime. However, those crimes that are so awful that they linger in men's memories, once proven, admit of no limitation on the period within which a prosecution must be brought in the case of a criminal who has sought to flee his punishment. But in lesser and insignificant crimes a time-limit ought to be set to save a citizen from uncertainty, because the long obscurity of the crime prevents its being an example of impunity to others, and the possibility remains of the guilty party's reforming in the interim. It is enough to point out these principles, because a limit can only be fixed with precision in relation to a particular code of laws and the given circumstances of a society. I shall merely add that, in a nation which has discovered the usefulness of moderate punishments, laws which extend or shorten the period available for prosecution in proportion to the gravity of the crime, using remand and voluntary exile as part of the punishment, will be able to provide a simple and restricted class of lenient punishments for a wide range of crimes.

But the periods in question shall not increase in direct proportion to the seriousness of the crime, since the likelihood of a crime is in inverse proportion to its seriousness. The period of investigation ought to diminish accordingly, therefore, and the time within which a prosecution must occur increase, which may seem to be in conflict with what I have said about equal punishments being given for unequal crimes if we count the period of remand or period of limitation before the verdict as part of the punishment. To clarify my idea for the reader, I distinguish two classes of crime: the first consists of serious crimes beginning with murder and including all the worst villainies; the second consists of minor crimes. This distinction has its foundation in human nature. The safety of one's own life is a natural right, the protection of property is a social right. The number of motives which impel men to overstep the natural feelings of pity is far fewer than the number of motives which impel them by the natural desire to be happy to violate a right which they do not find in their hearts but in social conventions. The vastness of the difference in probability of these two classes of crimes requires them to be regulated by different principles. In the most serious crimes, because they are the rarest, the period of enquiry should be decreased because of the greater likelihood that the accused is innocent, and the time set aside for preparation of the case ought to be increased, because the removal of the seductive prospect of impunity, which is the more harmful the more serious the crime, depends on a definitive verdict of innocence or guilt. But in minor crimes, since the accused's innocence is less likely, the time set aside for investigation should increase, and, since the harm caused by impunity is the less, the period for preparing the trial should decrease. Dividing crimes into two classes in this way would not be acceptable if the harm caused by crimes going unpunished decreased as the likelihood of guilt increased. {It might be recalled that an accused, who is found neither innocent nor guilty but who is discharged for lack of evidence, can be re-imprisoned and undergo a fresh investigation for the same crime if new and legally relevant evidence should turn up before the period of limitations for the crime has elapsed. At least this seems to me to be the proper attitude for the defence of both the subjects' security and their liberty. For it is too easy to favour either one of them at the expense of the other, so that each of these inalienable and equal prerogatives of every citizen goes unprotected and uncared for, the former in the face of overt or covert despotism and the latter in the face of turbulent popular anarchy.}

Chapter 31 Crimes difficult to prove

To someone who does not take into account the fact that reason has almost never been the lawgiver to nations, it will seem strange, in view of these principles, that crimes which are the most serious or the most fantastical and strange, that is, which are the least likely to occur, come to be proved by guesses or by the weakest and least clearcut evidence. It is as if the laws and the judge had an interest not in the truth, but in getting a guilty verdict; as if the conviction of an innocent man were not a greater danger the more the likelihood of innocence outstrips the likelihood of guilt. Most men lack the energy that is as necessary for great crimes as it is for great virtue, from which it seems that the two go together in those countries which sustain themselves more by the activity of government and a passion for the public good, than by their size or the constant high quality of their laws. In the latter sort of country, weakened passions seem better suited to maintaining than to improving the form of government. And from this we draw the important conclusion that great crimes do not always show that a country is in decline.

There are some crimes which are at once common in society and difficult to prove. And in these cases, the difficulty of producing evidence indicates the probability of innocence. And the harm of the crime's going unpunished being the less since the frequency of these crimes depends on principles other than the risk of being punished, so the time for investigation and the period allowed for prosecution should similarly be decreased. Yet adultery and sodomy which are hard crimes to prove, are precisely those in which, according to the received views, the tyrannical presumptions of the *nearly proofs* and *half-proofs* are admitted (as if a man could be *half-innocent* or *half-guilty*, that is, *half-punishable* or *half-acquittable*), and where, according to the cold and iniquitous teaching of some learned men who presume to offer norms and rules to the judiciary, torture exercises its cruel prerogatives on the body of the accused, the witnesses and even the whole family of the unfortunate.

Adultery is a crime which, viewed politically, is motivated and directed by two factors: the fluctuating laws of men and that very powerful attraction which urges one sex towards the other. This latter is similar in many respects to the gravitational forces that move the universe. Like gravity, it diminishes with distance, and, if the one rules all bodily movements, the other, so long as it lasts, rules all the movements of the soul. But sexual attraction differs from gravity in that gravity is counterbalanced by obstacles, whereas sex gathers strength and keenness the more obstacles are placed in its way.

If I were speaking to peoples still deprived of the light of religion, I would say that there is yet another difference between this crime and others. Adultery arises from the abuse of a constant and universal need in all mankind, a need antecedent to and, indeed, foundational of society itself, whereas other socially destructive crimes result from transitory emotions rather than natural need. To one who knows history and mankind, this need seems, in any given climate, to be always a constant quantity. Supposing this hypothesis to be true, then laws and mores which sought to decrease the total amount of such needs would be useless, even pernicious, because their effect would be to overload some people with the needs of others as well as their own. In contrast, they would be wise laws which, so to speak, by following the gentle slope of the plain, divided and split off the whole amount into as many equal and small parts, as were necessary to prevent drought or flood in every place. Conjugal fidelity is always proportional to the number and freeness of marriages. Where they are held together by ancestral prejudices, where they are welded and sundered by domestic power, there gallantry will stealthily break their bonds despite common morality, whose role it is to decry the effects and excuse the causes. But there is no need for such reflections for those who, living in the true religion, have higher motives, which correct the influence of natural impulses. The commission of such a crime is so instantaneous and mysterious, so covered by that very veil which the laws have set up, a necessary but fragile veil which raises rather than lowers the value of what it covers, the opportunities for crime are so easy, the consequences so equivocal, that the lawgiver has more chance of preventing it than of punishing it.

A general rule: for every crime which by its very nature generally goes unpunished, punishment becomes an incentive. It is a feature of our imagination that difficulties – so long as they are not insurmountable or excessively daunting to our natural laziness – tend to fire the imagination and make the object appear still more desirable. For those difficulties are like barriers which prevent the wandering and fickle imagination from leaving the object alone. Compelled to consider the object's every aspect, the imagination is led to attach itself to the pleasurable parts to which our souls are more naturally attracted than to the painful and unhappy, which they shun and flee.

Homosexuality, which is so severely punished by law and so easily subjected to the tortures which defeat innocence, has its foundation less in the needs of an isolated and free man, than in the emotions of a socialised and enslaved one. It derives its strength not so much from the satiation of pleasures as from that sort of education which begins by rendering men useless to themselves with a view to making them useful to others. It is a product of those houses where eager youth is cooped up and, deprived by insurmountable obstacles of all other contacts, expends its adolescent vigour in profitless activities, becoming old before its time.

Likewise, infanticide results from the unavoidable conflict in which a woman is placed if she has given in to weakness or violence. How could one who finds herself caught between disgrace and the death of a being unable to feel what harms it, not prefer the latter to the certain misery to which she and her unhappy fruit would be exposed? The best way to prevent this crime would be to have effective laws to protect the weak against the tyranny which exacerbates those vices which cannot cover themselves with the mantle of virtue.

I do not mean to belittle the just revulsion which these crimes deserve. But, having pointed out their sources, I think I am allowed to draw a general conclusion, which is that one cannot say that a punishment for a crime is exactly just (meaning necessary) until the law has instituted the best possible means in a given nation's circumstances for preventing such a crime.

Chapter 32   Suicide

Suicide is a crime which seems not to allow of being punished strictly speaking, since such a thing can only be visited either on the innocent or on a cold and insensible corpse. In the latter case, punishment would make no more impression on the living than whipping a statue. In the former case, it is unjust and tyrannical because man's political freedom presupposes that punishment be directed only at the actual culprit of a crime. Men love life too much and everything around them confirms them in this love. The enticing image of pleasure and hope, that sweetest snare of mortals, for which they will gulp down great draughts of evil if it is mixed with a few drops of delight, is too alluring for there to be any need to fear that the necessary impossibility of punishing such a crime will have any influence on men. He who fears pain obeys the law; but death extinguishes all the bodily sources of pain. What motive, then, can stay the desperate man's hand from suicide?

One who kills himself does less harm to society than one who leaves its borders forever; for the former leaves all his belongings, whilst the latter takes with him some part of what he owns. Indeed, if the strength of a nation consists in the number of its citizens, one who leaves a society to join a neighbouring nation does twice the harm of one who simply removes himself by death. The question then boils down to knowing whether it is useful or damaging to a country to allow its members a standing freedom to remove themselves beyond its borders.

No law should be issued which cannot be enforced or which the nature of the circumstances makes unenforceable. Since men are ruled by opinion, which obeys the slow and indirect pressure of the lawgiver, but resists measures which are abrupt or direct, so laws which are useless and scorned by men will bring into disrepute even the most salutary laws, which will come to be viewed as obstacles to be overcome rather than as the repository of the public good. Indeed, if, as we have said, our feelings are limited, the greater esteem men have for objects other than the laws, the less they will have for the laws themselves. From this principle the wise arranger of the public happiness can draw several useful conclusions, but setting them out would take us too far from our main topic, which is to show the pointlessness of turning a state into a prison. Such a law is pointless because, unless unscalable cliffs or impassable seas separate a country from all others, how can every point on its border be closed and how is one to guard the guards? Someone who takes everything with him cannot be punished. Once such a crime has been committed, it can no longer be punished; and punishing it beforehand is to punish men's will and not their actions, which would be to control the intentions, a part of a man utterly free from the reign of human laws. {{To punish the truant through the property he has left behind, even omitting the ease and inevitability of collusion, which could not be avoided without a tyrannical interference with contracts, would bog down all trade between nations.}} Punishing the criminal when he returns would prevent him from undoing the harm done to society by making all truancies permanent. The very ban on leaving a country breeds in the residents a desire to leave it, and is a warning to foreigners not to enter.

What should we think of a government which has no means but fear to prevent from leaving men who are naturally attached to their country since the earliest impressions of childhood? The surest way to bind men to their homeland is to raise the relative well-being of every one of them. Just as every effort ought to be made to keep the balance of trade in our favour, so the sovereign's and the nation's highest interest lies in ensuring that, compared with neighbouring countries, the total amount of happiness in the nation be greater than elsewhere. The pleasures of luxury are not the principal elements of this happiness, though they are a necessary remedy for inequality, which grows as the nation advances, as, without them, all the wealth would be concentrated in a single pair of hands. Where the borders of a country are extended more quickly than the population grows, luxury favours despotism. {{One reason for this is because, where there are fewer inhabitants, there is less industry, and where there is less industry, the poor are more dependent on the pomp of the rich, and the union of the oppressed against their oppressors is harder to organise and less to be feared. Another reason is because the homage, public offices, distinctions and deference which make the differences between the strong and the weak more obvious,}} can be more easily exacted from a few people than from many, since men are more independent when less observed and less observed when they are in larger numbers. But where the population grows more quickly than the borders do, luxury is opposed to the growth of despotism. For it stimulates men's industry and activity, and the accruing needs offer too many pleasures and comforts to rich men for them to be overly concerned with display, which is something that strengthens the sentiment of dependence, to play the major role in the economy. Therefore, we see that, unless some other factor is operative, in large, weak and underpopulated states the luxury of ostentation prevails over that of comfort; but in countries which are more populous than extensive, the luxury of comfort always diminishes ostentation. But commerce and the circulation of luxury goods has the unfortunate side-effect that, although it is carried out by the many, it arises from and ends up satisfying the pleasures of a few and the great majority of those involved enjoy only the smallest part of it. As a result, this trade does not choke off the feeling of poverty, which is caused more by relative differences than by real ones. But security and a freedom which is limited only by the laws are the main foundation of a nation's happiness; with them the pleasures of luxury benefit the people; without them they become instruments of tyranny. Just as the noblest animals and the freest birds flee to lonely places and impenetrable woods, and abandon the fertile and joyful fields where the huntsman lays his snares, so men refrain from pleasures themselves when tyranny offers them.

It is therefore established that the law which makes of its subjects prisoners in their own land is useless and unjust. Hence, so too will be any punishment for suicide; for even if it is a sin which God will punish, because only He can punish after death, it is not a crime before men, since the punishment, instead of falling on the malefactor, falls on his family. If it should be urged against me that such a punishment may nevertheless draw a man back from killing himself, I reply that one who calmly gives up the benefits of life, who so hates life herebelow as to prefer an eternity of sorrow, could hardly be prevailed upon by the less powerful and more distant thought of his children or relatives.

Chapter 33 Smuggling

Smuggling is a real crime against the sovereign and the nation, but the punishment of it should not involve dishonour since it does not seem disgraceful in the eyes of the public. If humiliating punishments are given to crimes which are not held to be dishonourable, then the feeling of disgrace aroused by those that really are so diminishes. One who sees the same punishment of death, for instance, for the killer of a pheasant as for the killer of a man or for the forger of an important document, cannot see any difference among these crimes. In this way the moral sentiments are destroyed, feelings which are the work of many centuries and much blood, and which are so slow and difficult to kindle in human hearts that it was believed necessary to employ the most sublime motives and the trappings of solemn ceremonial to arouse them.

This is a crime which arises from the law itself because the higher the custom duty, the greater the advantage; and so the temptation to smuggle and the ease of committing it grow as the borders to be protected lengthen and the volume of goods necessary for a profit diminishes. Punishment by confiscation of both the contraband goods and the gear found with it is very fair, but the lower the duty the more effective it would be, since men do not take risks except in proportion to the profit they expect to result from a successful venture.

But why does this crime not bring disgrace to its authors, given that it is a theft from the prince and so from the nation as a whole? My answer would be that crimes which men believe could not be visited on them personally do not interest them sufficiently to produce public outrage against the offenders. Smuggling is of this sort. Men, on whom its distant consequences make the slightest of impressions, do not see the harm which smuggling could do to them. Indeed, they often enjoy its immediate advantages. All they see is the harm done to the prince. They are not as concerned, therefore, to deny their good opinion to a smuggler as they are to a thief, a forger of signatures or those who commit other offences that might affect them directly. It is an evident principle that every sentient being is interested only in the harms which he knows.

But should such a crime go unpunished when the criminal has no possessions to lose? No: there are cases of smuggling which so closely affect the nature of taxation, which is so important and so intractable a part of good administration, that such a crime deserves a fairly heavy punishment, even up to imprisonment or penal servitude, but in such a way as to be fitting to the nature of the crime. For instance, the prison regime of a tobacco smuggler ought not to be the same as that of a hired assassin or a thief, and, to be the most fitting sort of punishment, his work ought to be limited to toil and exertion in the excise service which he wished to defraud.

Chapter 34　Of debtors

The need to guarantee the good faith of contracts and the security of trade require the lawgiver to assign to the creditors the persons of failed debtors. But I believe it is important to distinguish between the fraudulent bankrupt and the innocent bankrupt. The former ought to be punished with the same penalties which attach to the counterfeiter, because counterfeiting a metal coin, which is a token of the obligations citizens owe to each other, is no greater crime than counterfeiting the obligations themselves. {{But the innocent bankrupt is one who, after thorough investigation before his judges, has shown that he was stripped of his goods either by the wrong-doing of others, by the misfortune of others, or by circumstances beyond human control. On what barbarous grounds should he be thrown into prison, deprived of the sole, blighted good which is freedom, to suffer the miseries of the guilty, and, with the desperation of oppressed righteousness, perhaps go so far as to repent of his own innocence in which he lived peacefully under the protection of the laws, which it was beyond his power not to break? For these were laws dictated by the powerful out of greed and acquiesced in by the poor out of that hope which flickers in most human breasts and which makes us believe that events will be unfavourable to others and favourable to ourselves. Men's most superficial feelings lead them to prefer cruel laws. Nevertheless, when they are subjected to them themselves, it is in each man's interest that they be moderate, because the fear of being injured is greater than the desire to injure.

Returning to the innocent bankrupt, I admit that his obligations to his creditors should not be discharged until he has repaid them in full, that he should not be permitted to withdraw from them without the agreement of the interested parties nor to remove his business into another jurisdiction, when that business ought to be required under penalty to be so conducted as to put him back in a position to satisfy his creditors in proportion to the progress it makes. But what legitimate grounds, such as the security of trade or the sacred right to ownership, can possibly justify depriving him of his freedom? This would be useless except when the evils of servitude make the supposedly innocent bankrupt admit his guilt, a very rare case if the investigation has been thorough. I take it to be an axiom of lawgiving, that the weight to be given to the political disadvantages of the impunity of a given crime is in direct proportion to the harm done to the public and in inverse proportion to the likelihood of its being proved.

It should be possible to distinguish fraud from grievous culpability, the grievous from the mitigated culpability and this last from perfect innocence. To the first should be assigned the penalties for crimes of forgery, to the second lesser penalties, but including deprivation of freedom, and to the last should be reserved the free choice of the means to put himself back on his feet. In the third case, of mild fault, this choice should be left to the creditors. The distinctions between serious and mild offences should be fixed by blind and impartial laws, not by the dangerous and arbitrary discretion of judges. It is as necessary to fix limits in politics to measure the public good as it is in mathematics to measure quantities.[d]

How easily a farsighted lawgiver could prevent many culpable bankruptcies and repair the misfortune of the hardworking innocent! The public and open registration of all contracts, the freedom for all citizens to inspect the systematically ordered documentation, a

---

[d] {{Trade, or the ownership of goods, is not among the purposes of the social compact, but can be a means for achieving them. To expose the members of society to the harms to which so many occasions give rise, would be to subordinate the ends to the means, a mistake in every science but most of all in politics. I fell into this error in earlier editions, in which I said that the innocent bankrupt should be imprisoned as a pledge of his debts, or used as a slave in his creditors' employ. I am ashamed to have written in this way. I have been accused of irreligion and did not deserve it. I have been accused of subversiveness and did not deserve it. I have offended against the rights of man, and no-one has admonished me.}}

public bank founded on taxes wisely raised on flourishing trade and aimed at helping with appropriate funds unfortunate and innocent traders – these measures would have no real disadvantages and could produce innumerable advantages. But easy, simple and great laws, which await nothing but a sign from the lawgiver to spread prosperity and vigour throughout the nation, laws which would earn him immortal hymns of gratitude down the generations, are those which are least considered or least wanted. A nervous and nitpicking spirit, the fearful prudence of the present moment and an unadventurous dourness toward novelty take over the feelings of those who regulate the multifarious activities of little men.}}

Chapter 35 Asylums

Two questions remain to be considered: the first is whether it is just that there be places of asylum, and whether it is useful or not to have extradition treaties between different countries. Within a country's borders there should be no place which is outside the law. Its power should follow every citizen like a shadow. Impunity and asylum differ only in degree, and since the certainty of punishment makes more of an impression than its harshness, asylums invite men to commit crimes more than punishments deter them from them. To increase the number of asylums is to create so many little sovereign states, because where the law does not run, there new laws can be framed opposed to the common ones and there can arise a spirit opposed to that of the whole body of society. The whole of history shows that great revolutions, both in states and in the views of men, have issued forth from places of asylum. But as to whether extradition is useful I would not dare to say until there are laws better suited to human needs, and more lenient punishments that put an end to dependence on fickleness and mere opinion, so that persecuted innocence and despised virtue are protected; until tyranny has been banished to the vast plains of Asia by that universal reason which ever more closely unites the interests of the throne and its subjects. Nevertheless, the belief that there is no scrap of ground on which real crimes are tolerated would be an extremely effective way of preventing them.

Chapter 36 On setting a price on men's heads

The other question is whether it is useful to put a price on the head of a man known to be guilty and to make every citizen an executioner by arming him. The criminal is either outside or inside the country's borders. In the former case, the sovereign urges the citizens to commit a crime and exposes them to punishment for encroaching on and usurping the authority of other countries, and thereby authorises the other countries to do likewise to him. In the latter case, he shows his own weakness. If someone has the power to defend himself, he does not attempt to buy it. Moreover, such a decree overturns all ideas of morality and virtue, which are driven from the human mind by the slightest breeze. One moment the laws call for betrayal and the next they punish the same. With one hand the lawgiver tightens the bonds of family, of clan and of friendship, and with the other he rewards those who break and shatter them. Ever contradictory, one moment he urges the suspicious minds of men to have faith in each other, and the next he spreads misgivings in every heart. Instead of preventing one crime, he encourages a hundred. Such are the expedients adopted in weak nations, whose laws are nothing but makeshift repairs to a ruined building which is falling down on all sides. As enlightenment spreads through the nation, good faith and mutual assurance become the more necessary and tend to become inextricable from real politics. Chicanery, cabals and dark, twisted paths are mostly foreseen and the sensibility of all smothers the sensibility of each individual. The very centuries of ignorance, in which public morality compelled men to obey private morality, provide examples for the instruction and edification of enlightened centuries. But laws which reward betrayal and urge a clandestine war by sowing mutual mistrust among citizens run counter to this so essential union of morality and politics, which would bring happiness to humanity and peace to nations, and would bring to the world a longer period than it has ever enjoyed up until now of tranquillity and freedom from the evils that stalk its surface.

{Chapter 37   Attempted crimes, accomplices and immunity

Although the laws do not punish intentions, surely an action which shows a clear intent to commit a crime deserves to be punished, albeit less harshly than the actual execution of the crime would be. The necessity of preventing an attempt at crime justifies a punishment; but since the attempt and the carrying out of the crime may be separated by an interval, the heavier penalties for an accomplished crime might lead to a change of heart. The same may be said, although on different grounds, of a case in which there are accomplices in a crime, not all of whom are its main agents. When several men join together in a risky venture, the greater the risk, the more they try to share it equally among all of them. It will therefore be hard to find an individual prepared to be the main agent and to run a greater risk than his accomplices. The sole exception would be when the main agent is promised a special recompense. Since he would have been compensated for the greater risk he runs, in this case the penalty should be the same for all of them. Such considerations might seem too metaphysical to someone who does not recognise that it is of the greatest utility to have laws which elicit the fewest possible grounds for agreement among the participants in a crime.

Some courts offer free pardon to an accomplice in a serious crime who incriminates his partners. This sort of measure has its advantages and its disadvantages. The disadvantages are that the government licenses betrayal, which is hateful even among villains. For, crimes of courage are less ruinous to the nation than crimes of cowardice. The former are rare and only await a beneficent and

95

guiding hand to make them contribute to the public good. The latter are more common and infectious, and always more self-centred. Moreover, the court shows its own lack of resolve and the weakness of the law if it begs the help of those who offend against it. The advantages of such pardons are the possibility of preventing major crimes and the fact that they have an intimidating effect on the populace, since the agents remain hidden although the results of their confessions are obvious. In addition, it helps to show that whoever betrays the laws, which is to say the public, is likely to be unfaithful in private. It would seem to me preferable to have a general law promising immunity from prosecution to an accomplice who informs about any crime whatever, than to have a special dispensation for a particular case. Because in this way alliances between criminals could be discouraged by the mutual fear which each accomplice would have of exposing himself to danger; and the court would not be fuelling the audacity of villains by calling on their assistance in a particular case. Such a law, however, ought to join to banish the informer at the same time as pardoning him ... But I am torturing myself uselessly in trying to overcome the remorse which I feel in allowing betrayal and deception to be part of the sacrosanct laws, which are the foundation of public assurance, and the basis of human morality. What kind of example would it be to the nation if the promise of impunity were to be revoked and if someone who had simply responded to an invitation held out to him by the laws were to be dragged off to punishment as a result of some learned sophistry? Such examples are not rare among nations, and consequently not a few people think that a nation is nothing but a complicated machine whose levers are pulled at their pleasure by the most skilful and most powerful. Cold and indifferent to the delight of tenderer and sublimer souls, such men manipulate the dearest feelings and the most violent emotions with clinical precision when they see them useful to their own ends, playing on souls as musicians on their instruments.

Chapter 38 Leading interrogations, depositions

Our laws proscribe the use of *leading* questions in a trial, that is questioning which, according to the learned, asks about the *specifics*, when it should ask about the *general features* of the circumstances of a crime: questioning, in other words, which, being closely connected to the crime, *leads* the accused to give an immediate reply. According to theorists of the criminal law, questioning should, so to speak, spiral in on the facts and should never approach them directly. The grounds for this procedure are either so as not to *lead* an accused to implicate himself or perhaps because it seems to be unnatural that a suspect should accuse himself point blank.

Whichever of these two explanations is correct, there is a remarkable inconsistency in the laws between this convention and their sanctioning of torture; for what sort of interrogation could be more *leading* than pain? Examples of the first arise with torture, because the pain will *lead* the sturdy man to keep an obstinate silence and so exchange a heavier pain for a lighter; and it will *lead* the weak man to confess in order to free himself from the present pain which is so much more effective at that moment than future pain. The same goes for examples of the second kind, because if a *specific* question makes the guilty man confess against the rights of nature, agony will make him do so all the more easily. However, men are more impressed by the different names they give to things than by the actual differences between those things.

Among the other abuses arising from language and which have had no small influence on human affairs, we may note that which renders the deposition of a convicted criminal null and void. The traditional jurists gravely say that such a man is *legally dead*, and a *dead* man cannot perform any action. Many victims have been sacrificed to this fatuous metaphor; and it has often been seriously debated whether or not the truth should give way before juridical formulae. So long as the depositions of a convicted criminal do not go so far as to arrest the course of justice, why should the condemned man not be given the chance, even after the verdict has been handed down, in the name of the convict's extreme misery and the interests of truth, to bring forward new facts which change the nature of the case and can vindicate either himself or others with a new judgement? Formalities and ceremonials are necessary to the administration of justice, partly so that nothing is left to the discretion of the administrators, partly because they give people the idea of a judgement that is neither disorderly nor partial, but stable and regular, and partly because they make a bigger impression than argumentation would on men who are slavish followers of tradition. Truth, because it is either too simple or too complex, needs some pomp to recommend it to the ignorant multitude. But for the law to establish these ceremonies in ways which detract from the truth would be highly dangerous.

Finally, one who under examination obstinately refuses to answer the questions put to him, deserves a penalty which should be fixed by law, and be of the severest kind, in order to prevent men from avoiding their public duty in this way. Such a penalty is not called for when it is beyond doubt that a given suspect has committed a given crime, since in this case interrogations serve no useful purpose. Similarly, a confession is superfluous when other evidence proves an individual's guilt. This last is usually the case, because experience shows that on the whole the guilty deny everything.}

Chapter 39   Of a particular kind of crime

The reader of these pages will observe that I have said nothing about a particular sort of crime which once covered Europe with human blood and raised those sorry pyres whose flames were fed with the bodies of living men. These were times when the blind mob enjoyed the pleasing spectacle and sweet harmony of hearing muffled and chaotic groans issuing from swirling black smoke – smoke of human limbs, together with the cracking of charring bones and the frying of still-quivering organs. But reasonable men will see that neither the place, the time nor the present subject-matter allow me to discuss the nature of such a crime. It would take too long, and would take me too far from my topic to show, the example of many countries notwithstanding, how necessary perfect uniformity of thought ought to be in a state; how opinions, which differ only on a few very subtle and obscure points no human intelligence can grasp, can nevertheless overthrow the public good if one view is not preferred by authority to another; and how the nature of opinion is such that, whilst some opinions are clarified by being bandied and debated so that the true rise to the top and the false sink into oblivion, others, being insecure for all the steadfastness with which they are held, need to be arrayed in authority and power. It would take too long to show that, however hateful might seem the rule of force over the human mind, its only achievements being hypocrisy and hence moral degeneration; and however opposed to the spirit of kindness and fraternity which is enjoined by reason and by the authority we must revere, such a thing is nevertheless necessary and indispensable.

All the above must be believed as demonstrably true and in conformity with the real interests of men, if there is someone who carries it out with recognised authority. My topic is solely those crimes which arise from human nature and the social compact, and not those sins whose punishments, even in this life, ought to be regulated by principles other than those of a limited philosophy.

Chapter 40 False ideas of utility

One source of errors and injustices is the false ideas of utility held by some lawgivers. It is a false idea of utility that gives higher importance to particular inconveniences than to the general inconvenience, that commands the feelings instead of exciting them, that commands logic to submit. It is a false idea of utility that sacrifices a thousand real advantages for a single chimerical or unimportant disadvantage, that would deprive men of fire because it burns or water because it drowns, and can only remedy evils by destruction.

{{The laws which forbid men to bear arms are of this sort. They only disarm those who are neither inclined nor determined to commit crimes. Can it be supposed that those who have the courage to violate the most sacred laws of humanity and the most important in the civil code will respect the lesser and more arbitrary laws, which are easier and less risky to break, and which, if enforced, would take away the personal freedom – so dear to man and to the enlightened lawgiver – and subject the innocent man to all the annoyances which the guilty deserve? These laws make the victims of attack worse off and improve the position of the assailant. They do not reduce the murder rate but increase it, because an unarmed man can be attacked with more confidence than an armed man. These laws are not preventive but fearful of crime, they originate from the disturbing impression arising out of a few particular cases rather than from a reasonable consideration of the advantages and disadvantages of a universal law.}}

Similarly, a false idea of utility wishes to impose on a multitude of sentient creatures the symmetry and order of brute inanimate matter, and ignores the immediate motives, which alone work constantly and forcibly on the mass of people, in favour of remoter motives whose effect is very brief and weak, unless, that is, some power of the imagination, rare in human beings, compensates for the distance of their object by magnifying it.

Finally, it is a false idea of utility to sacrifice the thing to the name and to separate the public good from the good of each individual. The difference between the state of society and the state of nature is that savage man does not harm others except to benefit himself, whereas social man is sometimes moved by bad laws to offend against others without doing himself any good. The despot fills the souls of his slaves with fear and dejection, but these sentiments rebound on him with greater force to torture his own soul. The more solitary and domestic that fear is, the less it endangers whoever uses it as a means to his own happiness; but the more public it is, and the greater the number of men it inflames, the easier it becomes for a rash, desperate or daring man to compel others to serve his own ends, arousing in his followers feelings which are the more grateful and more enticing, the greater the number of men the risk falls upon. For the value which the oppressed place on their own lives decreases in proportion to the misery they are undergoing. This is the reason why offences cause new offences, for hatred is a more longlasting feeling than love, inasmuch as the former gathers strength from continued activity, which weakens the latter.

Chapter 41　How to prevent crimes

It is better to prevent crimes than to punish them. This is the principal goal of all good legislation, which is the art of guiding men to their greatest happiness, or the least unhappiness possible, taking into account all the blessings and evils of life. But the means hitherto employed have been mistaken or opposed to the proposed goal. The chaos of men's activities cannot be reduced to a geometric order devoid of irregularity and confusion. Just as the constant and very simple laws of nature do not prevent the planets being disturbed in their orbits, so human laws cannot prevent disturbances and disorders among the infinite and very opposite motive forces of pleasure and pain. Yet this is the fantasy of limited men when they have power in their hands. To forbid a large number of trivial acts is not to prevent the crimes they may occasion. It is to create new crimes, wilfully to redefine virtue and vice, which we are exhorted to regard as eternal and immutable. What a state would we be reduced to if we were forbidden everything which might tempt us to crime? It would be necessary to deprive a man of the use of his senses. For every motive which urges a man to commit a real crime, there are a thousand which urge him to perform those trivial actions which bad laws call crimes. And if the likelihood of crimes is proportional to the number of motives a man might have for them, broadening the range of crimes only increases the likelihood of their being committed. The majority of the laws are mere privileges, that is to say, a tribute from everyone for the comfort of the few.

Do you want to prevent crimes? Then make sure that the laws are clear and simple and that the whole strength of the nation is concentrated on defending them, and that no part of it is used to destroy them. {Make sure that the laws favour individual men more than classes of men.} Make sure that men fear the laws and only the laws. Fear of the law is salutary; but man's fear of his fellows is fatal and productive of crimes. Slavish men are more debauched, more sybaritic and crueller than free men. The latter ponder the sciences and the interests of the nation, they envisage and aspire to great things; but the former are content with the present moment and seek amid the din of depravity a distraction from the emptiness of their everyday lives. Accustomed to uncertainty about the result of everything, the result of their crimes becomes doubtful to them, reinforcing the emotions by which they are driven. In a country which is idle by virtue of its climate, uncertainty in its laws maintains and increases the country's idleness and stupidity. If a country is debauched but energetic, uncertainty in its laws will waste the country's energy in the formation of numberless little cabals and intrigues, which spread suspicion in every heart and make betrayal and pretence the basis of good sense. If a country is brave and strong, uncertainty eventually will be removed, though only after the nation has passed through many fluctuations from freedom to slavery and from slavery to freedom.

Chapter 42 The sciences

Do you want to prevent crimes? Then see to it that enlightenment and freedom go hand in hand. The evils which arise from knowledge are in inverse proportion to its diffusion, and the benefits are in direct proportion. A daring impostor, who is always an uncommon man, wins the adoration of an ignorant people and the jeers of an enlightened one. By facilitating the making of comparisons and multiplying the points of view, knowledge counterposes different sentiments, which modify each other reciprocally, a process that becomes all the easier as we learn to anticipate the same views and the same objections in others. In the face of widespread enlightenment within a nation, foul-mouthed ignorance is silenced and the authority which has no defences in reason trembles. Only the vigour of the laws remains unshaken. For there is no enlightened man who does not love the public, clear and useful compacts that guarantee the common security, comparing that small portion of useless freedom that he has sacrificed with the sum of the freedoms sacrificed by others who, without the laws, could become conspirators against him. Looking upon a well-framed code of laws and finding that he has lost nothing but the sorry freedom to do harm to others, any sensitive soul will be compelled to bless the throne and its occupant.

It is not true that the sciences are always harmful to mankind, and, that when they have been so, it was an evil men could not avoid. The increase of the human species across the face of the Earth introduced war, the cruder arts, and the first laws, which were the temporary pacts which arose and perished with the necessity of the moment. This was man's first philosophy, whose few elements were just, because his idleness and small wisdom saved him from mistakes. But the needs of men increased with the increase of their numbers. Stronger and more lasting impressions were therefore called for to save men from repeated returns to the original state of unsociability, which was becoming ever more ruinous. Those first errors which populated the Earth with false gods and set up an invisible universe which regulated ours were therefore of great benefit to humanity (I mean a great political benefit). It was an act of kindness to men to dazzle them with supernatural wonders and to drag docile ignorance to the altars. By presenting men with objects beyond their senses, which fled before them just as they believed they were within their grasp, which were never despised, because never really known, they united men's divided emotions and focussed them on a single object which strongly absorbed them. These were the first events which lifted all nations out of the savage state. This was the age when great societies were formed, and such was the nature of the bond, perhaps the only bond needed to bind them. I do not speak of God's Chosen People, for whom the most extraordinary miracles and the most marked favours took the place of human politics. But as it is a feature of error to divide itself *ad infinitum*, the sciences which were born out of error turned men into a blind and fanatical mob who, caught in a maze ran into each other and muddled each other to such an extent that some sensitive and philosophic souls went so far as to regret the ancient state of savagery. This is the first age in which knowledge, or at least opinion, is harmful.

The second age consists in the difficult and terrifying passage from error to truth, from unknowing darkness to enlightenment. The mighty clash between errors useful to a few powerful men and the truths useful to many weak men, the coming together and the agitation of emotions which such an occasion prompts, add innumerable evils to the suffering of mankind. Whoever reflects on the various histories of nations, which after a certain lapse of time come to resemble each other in their main outlines, will repeatedly find a whole generation sacrificed to the happiness of succeeding generations in the hard-fought but necessary transition from the shadows of ignorance to the light of philosophy and, as a corollary, in the passage from tyranny to freedom. But once men's souls have calmed and the fires which purged the nation of the evils which oppressed it have cooled, then truth, whose progress accelerates after the first slow steps, shall sit on the throne as the consort of the monarch, and shall be worshipped and have an altar in the parliaments of republics. Who then will be able to say that the light which illuminates the multitude is more harmful than the shadows, or that a good understanding of the true and simple relations of things can ever be ruinous to men?

If blind ignorance is less lethal than mediocre and confused knowledge, since the latter adds to the former the inevitable mistakes of one who has a limited vision even within the bounds of truth, the greatest gift a sovereign can give the nation and himself would be to make an enlightened man the repository and the guardian of the sacred laws. Accustomed to looking fearlessly at the truth, lacking most of the unexamined and insatiable urges that stand in the way of virtue in most men, habituated to viewing humanity from the highest vantage points, his nation becomes a family of brothers. And the more of mankind he has before his eyes, the shorter the distance separating the great from the mass of people seems to him. Philosophers have needs and interests which are unknown to common folk, in particular that of not denying in public the principles which they preach in private, and they acquire the habit of loving truth for its own sake. A pick of such men fashions the happiness of the nation; but it is a fleeting happiness if good laws do not so increase their numbers as to diminish the always significant likelihood of a bad selection.

Chapter 43 Magistrates

Another way of preventing crimes is to make the tribunal charged with executing the laws more interested in observing the laws than in corrupting them. The more men make up this body the smaller the danger of the laws being usurped. For it is harder to bribe officers who keep an eye on each other, and they have less interest in increasing their own power the smaller the portion that each has of it, especially when compared with the risks involved in such an effort. If, by pomp and display, the harshness of his edicts and his refusal to hear the just or unjust petitions of those who suppose themselves ill-used, the sovereign accustoms his subjects to fear the magistrates more than the laws, then the magistrates will profit from this fear more than personal and public safety will gain.

Chapter 44 Public awards

Another means of preventing crimes is to reward virtue. I notice that the laws of all nations today are totally silent on this matter. If the prizes given by academies to the discoverers of useful truths have increased both knowledge and the number of good books, why should not prizes distributed by the beneficent hand of the sovereign likewise increase the number of virtuous actions? In the hands of the wise distributor, the coin of honour will prove a lasting investment.

Chapter 45 Education

Finally, the surest but hardest way to prevent crime is to improve education. This topic is too broad and goes beyond the limits which I have set myself. It is a topic, I dare to add, which is too intertwined with the nature of government for it to be left an untilled field, and only cultivated here and there by a few wise men until the distant future when public happiness reigns. A great man, who enlightens mankind even as it persecutes him, has shown in detail the principal precepts of an education which is truly useful to men. It consists less in a sterile mass of subjects than in the precise and informed choice of topics; it replaces copies with originals in the study of both the physical and moral phenomena which either chance or effort presents to fresh young minds. It encourages virtue by the easy path of the feelings, and diverts men away from evil by the infallible method of alerting them to the necessary ill consequences it brings, rather than by the uncertain method of ordering them what to do, which gains only a feigned and fleeting obedience.

{{Chapter 46   Pardons

As punishments become milder, clemency and pardons become less necessary. Happy the nation in which they are harmful! Clemency, then, a virtue which has often complemented all the duties which attach to the sovereign's throne, should be redundant in a perfect administration where punishments are mild and the methods of judgement are regular and expeditious. This truth will seem hard to one who lives amid the chaos of a criminal system in which amnesties and pardons are called for in proportion to the absurdity of the laws and the awful severity of the sentences. Clemency is the most beautiful prerogative of the throne, it is the most desirable endowment of sovereignty and it is the tacit condemnation which the benevolent dispensers of the public happiness make of a code of laws which, for all its imperfections, has on its side the prejudice of ages, the voluminous and impressive tomes of innumerable commentators, the staid paraphernalia of endless procedural formalities, and the support of the most fawning and least feared semi-literates. But one ought to bear in mind that clemency is a virtue of the lawgiver and not of the laws' executor, that it ought to shine in the legal code and not in particular judgements. To show men that crimes can be pardoned, and that punishment is not their inevitable consequence, encourages the illusion of impunity and induces the belief that, since there are pardons, those sentences which are not pardoned are violent acts of force rather than the products of justice. What will be said, then, of a prince who offers a pardon, that is, public safety to an individual and, with a private act of unenlightened kind-heartedness, makes a public decree of impunity?

The laws, therefore, ought to be inexorable and so should their executors in particular cases. But the lawgiver ought to be gentle, lenient and humane. The lawgiver ought to be a skilled architect, who raises his building on the foundation of self-love, and the interest of all ought to be the product of the interests of each. As a result, he shall not be required to separate the public good from the good of individuals with partial laws and disorderly remedies, and to raise a false image of public well-being on fear and suspicion. As a deep and sensitive philosopher, he ought to let men, his brothers, enjoy in peace that small portion of happiness which is set aside for them to enjoy in this corner of the universe by the huge system set up by the First Cause, by He Who Is.}}

Chapter 47   Conclusion

I conclude with a final reflection that the severity of punishments ought to be relative to the state of the nation itself. Stronger and more easily felt impressions have to be made on a people only just out of the savage state. A lightning strike is needed to stop a fierce lion who is provoked by a gunshot. But as souls become softened by society, sensitivity grows. And as it does so, the severity of punishments ought to diminish, if the relation between the object and the sensation is to remain constant.

From all I have written it is possible to draw a very useful general axiom, though it little conforms to custom – the most usual legislator of nations. It is: *In order that punishment should not be an act of violence perpetrated by one or many upon a private citizen, it is essential that it should be public, speedy, necessary, the minimum possible in the given circumstances, proportionate to the crime, and determined by the law.*

To Jean Baptiste D'Alembert[1]

Milan

24 August 1765

Forgive me, sir, if I take the liberty of writing to you; it is a consequence of the feelings of esteem, regard and admiration that I have for perhaps the greatest genius of this enlightened century. I did not need to learn of the praise you so kindly gave of my work in your letter to Father Frisi, in order to discover it in my heart. It is you, sir, who have been my master; it is from your works that I drew the spirit of philosophy and humanity which pleased you in my book; it is yours more than you think. I never weary of reading the Preface to the *Encyclopaedia*, the *Elements of Philosophy*; in short, sir, your works are the daily nourishment of my soul. How I envy and admire in you the creative spirit, which seems to be superior even to the most sublime truths which it communicates to us! While I was writing my book, before my existence was known to you, how many times did I flatter myself that one day it would come into the hands of a d'Alembert! My ambition is fulfilled, and I would have to borrow the tongue of flatterers if I were to render to you, sir, all the respect and regard I feel for you. The approval which you so kindly expressed is such an honour for me that it is the greatest reward I could receive, after that of saving some innocent victim from the hands of tyranny. It has moved me, sir, and encourages me to go on with my career

---

[1] Beccaria's letter, written in French, was occasioned by d'Alembert's favourable comments on his book in a letter of 9 July 1765 to the Milanese mathematician Paolo Frisi.

115

and to make myself worthy of your esteem. In this way, in a foreign land, in the very midst of Spanish prejudices which ring in my ears, the genius of the great d'Alembert encourages and supports in a career of public usefulness a soul which, left to itself, would restrict itself to cultivating philosophy in peace and obscurity.

I have read with admiration your work on the Jesuits,[2] a well-worn subject, which, in your hands, sir, has taken on an air of novelty: it contains that philosophical spirit which charms, which clarifies and which allows the reader to draw many conclusions. You know, sir, that when one discusses such matters with the impartiality of a philosopher; when one dares to discuss these miserable controversies, the shame and the scourge of weak humans, in terms which are worthy of you, sir; when one retains neutrality between two parties which vie with each other in declaring that *Qui non est mecum contra me est*;[3] you better than anyone know, I say, that such a work is bound to have enemies: but it is bound to have admirers for all time; it is destined to immortalise the name of the Jesuits, and it will teach the most distant posterity what a powerful body, or a state, can do, even if it has no force, so long as it knows how to manage people's opinions. One day the same impression will be made by your work on posterity as would be made on us today if Tacitus had left us a treatise on the intrigues and the influence which the soothsayers of his time wielded over the republic. Philosophers see no harm in the Jesuits other than in their effect on humanity and the sciences. The vulgar and especially the prejudiced only hate them from an envy and jealousy born out of conspiracy and intrigue at an organisation which overshadows them.

My self-esteem is very flattered, sir, by the translation which is going to be done under your auspices; I take the liberty of sending you, sir, a few additions which I have made to it and which will shortly be included in the new edition coming out in Italy.[4] I shall be even more indebted to you than I am already if you will be so

---

[2] D'Alembert's *Sur la destruction des Jésuites en France* (1765) had been published anonymously and was attacked by the Jesuits and by their opponents the Jansenists (by whom d'Alembert had been educated).
[3] In Latin in the original: 'Who is not with me is against me', see Matthew 12:30 and Luke 11:32.
[4] Beccaria is referring to the additions to the fifth edition – see Note on the text for *On Crimes*.

good as to pass them on to the philosopher[5] who is honouring me by translating the book. I am asked by my good friend, Count Verri, to send you his respects and his most sincere thanks for the favourable reception you kindly extended to his discourse on happiness.[6]

I remain, etc.,
Cesar Beccaria

[5] André Morellet, see next letter pp. 119–20.
[6] D'Alembert had written appreciatively of Pietro Verri's *Meditazioni sulla felicità* (1763) in the letter to Paolo Frisi referred to in note 1 above.

To André Morellet[1]

Allow me, sir, to address you with the formulae in common use in your language, which are the most convenient, the simplest, the truest and so the most worthy of a philosopher such as you. Allow me also to make use of a copyist, the letter which I wrote you being barely legible. The charming letter you so kindly wrote to me excited in me feelings of the deepest respect, the greatest regard and the liveliest friendship. I cannot know how to express to you how honoured I felt on hearing my work had been translated into your language – the language of the nation that enlightens and instructs all Europe. I myself owe everything to French books. They developed in my soul the sentiments of humanity which had been stifled by eight years of fanatical and servile education.[2] I already regard your name with respect because of the excellent articles you contributed to that immortal work, the *Encyclopaedia*;[3] and it was the pleasantest surprise possible for me to discover that a scholar of your reputation had condescended to translate my book.[4] I thank you with all my heart for the gift you have made

---

[1] Beccaria's letter is a reply to Morellet's of 3 January 1766. Morellet wrote to introduce himself, enclosing a copy of his translation of *On Crimes*, and explaining the changes he had made to it.

[2] From 1746 to 1754, Beccaria was at the Jesuit boarding school, the Collegio Farnesiano in Parma.

[3] Morellet says in his letter, that the main articles he contributed were on Fate (*Fatalité*), Shape (*Figure*), the Son of God (*Fils de Dieu*), Faith (*Foi*), and on the Gomarists, among others which appeared in volume VII.

[4] A surprise because Beccaria was unaware of the translation prior to its completion. In his *Mémoires*, Morellet recalls having been asked at a dinner with de Malesherbes

me with your excellent translation and with your thoughtfulness in satisfying my curiosity so promptly. I have read it with inexpressible pleasure, and found that you have improved on the original. I can affirm in all sincerity that the order which you have followed seems to me to be more natural than and hence preferable to my own, and that I am vexed that the new Italian edition is close to being finished, because I should have adapted it to conform entirely, or almost entirely, to your plan.[5] You have, sir, done extremely well in leaving out the eulogy of the professor, who is Dr Soria, a famous man in Italy. This was inserted by the printer, who is a friend of his, and I was unable to prevent it; nor could I do anything about the reply to the friar, which was simply intended to protect me from the hurricane he was calling down on my head. My work has lost none of its power in your translation, except for those discrepancies that arise from the intrinsic differences between the two languages. The main difference, it seems to me, is that Italian is a suppler and more malleable language, and perhaps at the same time a less cultivated one, so that certain turns of phrase are possible in it that would perhaps offend the taste of a more cultured nation. I see no substance in the objection which was made to you, that the change of order might weaken some of the book's power. Its power consists in the choice of expressions and in the bringing together of ideas, and confusion can only undermine these two effects. Nor should fear of wounding the author's self-esteem have stopped you. First of all, because, as you yourself rightly say in your excellent preface, once a book which pleads the cause of humanity is published, it belongs to the world and to every nation; and, as for myself, I would have made precious little progress in the philosophy of the heart, which I place above that of the intellect, if I had not learnt to have the courage to face the truth. I hope that the fifth Italian edition, which ought to be appearing soon, will soon be sold out, and I assure you that in the sixth I shall observe entirely, or almost entirely, the new order, which makes the truths gathered in the book shine forth still more

to translate the difficult first sentence of the book. He then borrowed the volume, and had translated the rest six weeks later.

[5] For details of Morellet's alterations, Beccaria's response to them, and their profound consequences for the subsequent reception of his book, see the Note on the text.

clearly and brightly. I say 'almost entirely' because, after the single eager read-through which I have given it so far, I cannot make as thorough judgement of the details as I already can of the whole. My close friends' impatience to read your beautiful translation compelled me, sir, to allow it to go out of my hands as soon as I had read it, and I am obliged to put off to another letter the explanation of some passages which you find obscure. But I can say that, in writing it, I had before me the examples of Machiavelli, Galileo and Giannone. I could hear the rattling chains of superstition and the howls of fanaticism stifling the faint moans of truth. It was this that caused me – forced me – sometimes to veil the light of truth in a pious shroud. I wished to defend humanity without being a martyr to it. The habitual caution instilled in me by the need to express myself obscurely has sometimes made me do so even when I did not need to.

To this must be added my literary inexperience – I am only twenty-eight years old and just five as a writer.

Words cannot express, sir, the joy with which I regard the interest you take in me and how touched I am by the signs of esteem which you show me, signs which I cannot accept without appearing vain nor reject without offending you. I was equally abashed by the obliging things which you pass on to me from those matchless philosophers who do honour to humankind, Europe and their nations – d'Alembert, Diderot, Helvétius, Buffon and Hume: what illustrious, what stirring names! Your immortal works are my constant reading, the object of my studies during the day and of my meditations at night. How could I, filled with the truths you teach, praise the errors which are worshipped and abase myself so far as to lie to posterity? What I write to you, sir, is exactly what I feel. I find myself repaid beyond my hopes in receiving signs of respect from all these famous men whom I consider my teachers. I beg you to convey my humblest thanks to each in turn and to assure them that I bear towards them the deep and true respect that any sensitive soul must feel for truth and virtue. I beg you to assure Baron d'Holbach of the deep reverence, gratitude and esteem I feel for him and of my keen desire that he should find me worthy of his friendship.

You and your friends do me too great an honour in your enquiries regarding my life. I shall do my best to satisfy your curiosity in all sincerity. I am the eldest son of a family which owns some property; but various circumstances, some necessary and some depending on the will of others, do not leave me very well off. I have a father whose age and even whose prejudices I have to respect. I am married to a sensitive young woman who loves to cultivate her mind, and I have the rare happiness to add the tenderest friendship to love. I have no occupation other than that of peacefully cultivating philosophy – something that allows me to satisfy three of my liveliest feelings: love for renown, love for freedom, and compassion for the misfortunes of men oppressed by error. I set the date of my conversion to philosophy as five years ago, and I owe it to the reading of the *Persian Letters*. The second book which wrought a revolution in me was by M. Helvétius. It was he who pushed me powerfully in the direction of the truth and who first awoke my attention to the blindness and misfortunes of mankind. I owe a large portion of my ideas to the reading of *On Spirit*. The sublime work of M. de Buffon opened to me the sanctuary of nature. I read the whole of the twelfth and thirteenth quarto volumes in which I especially admired the two views of nature, which carried me away by the philosophical eloquence with which they are written. What I have been able to read to date by M. Diderot, namely, the dramatic works, the *Interpretation of Nature* and the articles in the *Encyclopaedia*, has seemed to me to be filled with ideas and passion. What a wonderful man he must be! Mr Hume's profound metaphysics and the truth and novelty of his views astonished and enlightened my mind. I have recently read the eighteen volumes of his history with endless pleasure. I have seen in it a political thinker, a philosopher and an historian of the first order. What should I say to you of the philosophical works of M. d'Alembert? They show an immense chain of great and new ideas, and I find in them the loftiness of mind and the style of a legislator. His Preface to the *Encyclopaedia* and his *Elements of Philosophy* are classic works and contain within them the seeds of an infinity of future researches. I know enough mathematics to appreciate this famous man's great discoveries and to regard him as this century's greatest geometer. I have also derived a great deal of instruction from the works of the abbé de Condillac. In my view, these are masterpieces of precision, clarity and good metaphysics. I eventually had the honour of meeting him in Milan and of making friends with him. I lead a quiet and solitary life, if one can call solitude the company of a select circle of friends, who provide constant stimulation to both heart and mind. We follow the same studies and the same pleasures. That is my resource and what prevents me from feeling an exile in my own land.

This country is still buried under the prejudices which its ancient masters left it. The Milanese do not forgive those who wish them to live in the eighteenth century. In a capital of 120,000 inhabitants, there are hardly twenty individuals who desire to instruct themselves and who devote themselves to truth and virtue. My friends and I are convinced that journals are one of the best ways to get those who are incapable of any serious application to read a little; we publish a sheet on the model of *The Spectator*,[6] which has done so much in England to add to the culture of the mind and to the progress of good sense. I shall be honoured to send you a collection of this material. You will find some of it bad, some mediocre and some good. It includes the following pieces by me: an essay on smells, a fragment on style, a discussion of periodical publishing, another on the pleasures of the imagination and a translation of a piece by de Montmort on games of chance. These are all things written with the haste which goes into periodical publications. The items by Count Verri are marked with the letter 'P'. He is already known to you for his wonderful little *Treatise on Happiness*. He is an outstanding man for the qualities of his heart and of his mind, and he is the dearest of my friends. It seems to me that I feel for him the same fervent friendship which Montaigne felt for Etienne de la Boetie. It is he who encouraged me to write and it is to him that I owe my not having thrown into the fire the manuscript of *On Crimes* which he kindly copied out himself in his own hand.

Literature has lost a thinker, but the nation has gained an excellent minister, in the person of Count Carli, who is known for a work on monetary reform, and who has just been made chairman

---

[6] Beccaria was one of the contributors to *Il caffè*, which was meant to appear every ten days. It ran, under Pietro Verri's editorship, from June 1764 to June 1766. Beccaria wrote an article on journals for *Il caffè* in 1765, where he once again expressed his admiration for *The Spectator*. *The Spectator* was an English periodical run from 1711 to 1712 by Sir Richard Steele (1672–1729) and Joseph Addison (1672–1719). It effectively established the essay as a form suited to a wide readership.

of an economic council newly set up in our town. He will be a philosophical minister, and that is to say everything.

You will, sir, forgive me all these details; you wrote to me in all candour and I have to reply in kind; you have set the example and I must imitate you. My other friends are a brother of Count Verri, who like him is very talented, Marquess Longo, Count Visconti, Signor Lambertenghi, Count Secchi, etc.[7] Together we cultivate in solitude and silence that true philosophy which was previously regarded here with suspicion and contempt. Believe me, sir, that the French philosophers have a colony of true disciples in this America of ours, disciples because disciples of reason. You may, therefore, judge how grateful and pleased I shall be to receive the works of which you give notice which are a source of instruction and consolation to all of humanity.[8] What generosity on your part to have taken such notice of my book and for your kindness in having interrupted an immense and interesting project[9] to concern yourself with a translation. And you will forgive me for observing that your folio volumes cannot be those which no-one reads. The *Encyclopaedia* and my copy of Bacon are in folio, and your work will be of the same standing. I send you a million thanks for the copies of the translation which you attach to your works. I am already overwhelmed by your generosity, but must ask you one more kindness: that of sparing me the remorse of having been the cause of expense on your part.

My friends and I have the highest regard for Gatti's excellent work which you have translated. I should not have been able to read it if the abbé de Condillac had not sent me it from Parma: French books are extremely hard to come by here, especially recently published ones (a fact that has sadly deprived me of the pleasure of reading and admiring your other works). Gatti's work I found full of a philosophical spirit which is very rare in medical

---

[7] This is a partial roll-call of the Accademia dei pugni.

[8] In the letter to which Beccaria is replying, Morellet had promised to send some books and pamphlets which he had written and translated. Two concern trade and industry in France; two others concern the Inquisition and censorship; and one, referred to by Beccaria below, is Morellet's translation of a work written in Paris in 1763 on inoculation by the Pisan medical theorist Angelo Giuseppe Maria Gatti (1730–98).

[9] A dictionary of commerce and economics, of which only a prospectus was issued in 1769.

books. If my circumstances allowed it, I would fly to Paris to educate myself, to marvel at you, to express to you in person all that I feel for you, for d'Alembert and for your illustrious friends. I nevertheless hope that my circumstances will change and that this delay will put me in a state worthier of your society. In the meantime, you say that your brother is planning to visit Milan?[10] I hope he will do me and my friends the honour of allowing us to do what we can to make his stay in our town as little tiresome as is possible.

In the meantime, feel free to ask anything you want of me, without constraint, as one philosopher to another; and allow me the privilege of becoming your correspondent in Italy. Your friends may also avail themselves of me, and I desire that they should do me this honour. The feelings you have expressed towards me, those of your friends and those of Baron d'Holbach, fill me with a gratitude which will end only with my life, and I assure you that my words are no match for what I feel for you. I beg you to thank on my behalf and in the warmest possible terms Monsieur Helvétius, Diderot, Buffon, Hume and d'Holbach, who have so signally honoured me, and to ask them to allow me to send them copies of the new edition of my book. I am writing to d'Alembert myself. Count Firmian came back to us in Milan a few days ago, but he is very busy and I have not been able to see him yet. I shall not forget to give him your regards. He has protected my book and it is to him that I owe my peace of mind.

I shall soon send you some explanation of the passages which you found obscure, and which are unforgivable, because I did not write not to be understood by philosophers like yourself. I beg you to send me your observations and those of your distinguished friends in all haste and in complete frankness, so that I may make use of them for a sixth edition. Send me, above all, the results of your conversations with M. Diderot about my book. I ardently wish to know what impression I have made on that sublime soul. I am sending you the book by the Vallombrosian monk called Vincenzo [*sic*] Facchinei of Corfu. This man wanted to gain the favour of the Venetian Republic by attacking a book which had been very

---

[10] Morellet's brother was acting as tutor on a tour of Italy to Louis Alexandre, duc de Rochefoucauld d'Enville, grandson of the moralist.

harshly proscribed, in the belief that the book came from the pen of a Venetian subject involved in the opposition to the state inquisitors in the recent troubles which took place in Venice.[11] Therefore I am sending this critique, our journal and another little pamphlet on currency reform[12] which, though it is the work of my youth, I ought not to hide from a man like you, who honours me with his friendship.

I stop here to allow my letter to go by tomorrow's courier. I beg you to send me a word of reply, because I am very impatient to know whether these inadequate expressions of my gratitude, respect and friendship have reached you. I have the honour to remain . . .

Milan
26 January 1766

P.S. I once again crave forgiveness for my impertinence and for the copyist I have used.

I write this postscriptum from the house of the Countess della Somaglia, née Belgioioso, a lady of the finest qualities of mind and heart, full of virtue, sensitivity and learning. You must have met her here in Milan; in the first years of her marriage, she cut one the most brilliant figures in Paris.

Father Frisi, the well-known mathematician, asks me to convey to you his compliments. He greatly esteems you. He is one of my dearest friends. He may be going to Paris in the Spring. How I envy his good fortune!

I have just heard of Mr Hume's gesture towards M. Rousseau, which does honour to philosophy and to philosophers.[13] How sweet it would be to be able to imitate it!

I heard yesterday evening that they are reprinting your translation of my book at Yverdon.

[11] The troubles arose from an attempt by a Venetian noble, Angelo Querini (1721–96), to use the relatively unimportant legal office of Avogadore di Comun to undermine the position of the inquisitors and of the Ten, who ruled Venice. He was jailed in 1763.

[12] His pamphlet *Del disordine e de' rimedi delle monete nello Stato di Milano nell'anno 1762* (Lucca, 1762).

[13] Hume offered Rousseau asylum in England in late 1765 following his condemnation in France (1762), Geneva (1763) and Berne (1764).

Excuse, sir, my scribble and my bad French phrasing.

I desire your friendship and shall make every effort to deserve it. My specific comments on your excellent translation will be a little late, for Count Firmian, among others, will want to admire your translation without delay, and I must, of course, comply. Sadly, this will mean that I shall have to delay the pleasure of demonstrating to you in full my eagerness to obey your commands. Once again, I am with the greatest affection

Beccaria

Inaugural Lecture[1]

I have been honoured by Her Imperial Majesty[2] with an appointment to teach public economy and commerce: that is to say, those sciences which can indicate to us the means for conserving, increasing and exploiting to the full the wealth of a state. Although I have serious doubts about whether my powers are equal to the task of addressing so vast a subject, I am comforted and reassured by having to perform this duty in my own country, where at least I shall be called on neither to conceal the truth under a veil of artifice, nor to seek my examples only in far-off places or in the musty pages of neglected authors. On the contrary, a quick glance at what has been done in this fortunate province, provides countless glorious past instances and present proofs of the most important and useful truths of public economy. The lands have been properly assessed, the taxes are fair and manufacturing is encouraged, magistracies have been set up to take especial care of the nation's riches and the sciences, and great benefits have been heaped on the nation's subjects. Among the most striking instances of our august sovereign's favour, one of the greatest is undoubtedly the choice of that illustrious personage who heads the affairs of this state.[3] He is a person no less versed in the profoundest reflections of literature than the wisest maxims of good government, while the

---

[1] This lecture was delivered on 9 January 1769, and inaugurated Beccaria's course of lectures on public economy which he delivered as part of his duties as the newly created Professor of Cameral Sciences at the Palatine School in Milan.
[2] Empress Maria Theresa (1717–80)
[3] I.e., Count Carlo di Firmian.

noblest virtues of affability, humanity and equanimity shine forth all the more for being found in one of so high a rank.

Under so mild and enlightened an administration, protected by the triumphal shadow of the imperial laurels, the humble and peaceable laurels of the Muses no longer wither and decay, but put forth new shoots and gain in strength. And Cardano's homeland witnesses the rebirth of the arts and sciences; without which the yielding but tumultuous folly of the people either stagnates in sterile inactivity or is dragged along in the wake of ruinous prejudices.

The throne has not yet issued all its provisions concerning so important a matter. In the meantime, it has been graciously commanded that instruction be given, in the common language, in the science which at one time was with useless, or rather harmful, caution withheld from public scrutiny. This was a serious miscalculation, especially since all the sciences, and especially the political sciences, grow and become clearer as they are subjected to vigorous discussion amongst different intellects, and when their light shines universally, public opinion becomes a curb on potential abuses. Furthermore, the wisest dispositions are frequently opposed by a thousand prejudices which poison the subjects' minds against the most sincere and beneficial decisions; and the most useful, and therefore most feared, innovations are resisted by ridiculous fears, by malevolent biasses, and by errors which are sheltered by sterile habit; moreover, with the spread of enlightenment among ordinary people, these malevolent gremlins disappear and the obedience which is due to orders from on high becomes readier and gladder because it is spontaneous and reasoned.

It is clear, then, how publicly useful a thing it is that these sciences should be supported by the public authorities and cultivated by those citizens who aim to make themselves fit to be entrusted by the sovereign with the zealous care of the interests of the principality and the nation.

No one should believe that blind experience and mechanical habit can take the place of sure principles and of reasoned maxims in confronting unexpected political circumstances. Nor is it enough to have general truths without descending to particulars, since theory, in these sciences, often has to be profoundly and substantially modified in the light of attempts to apply it to individual cases. For example, it is necessary not only to know that commerce flourishes as a result of four main factors, namely, competition in the prices of goods, an economy of labour, cheap transport, and low interest rates; or that industry is stimulated and invigorated by low duties on the import of raw materials and the export of finished goods, and by raising duties on the import of finished goods and on the export of raw materials; or that all economic operations boil down to the securing of the largest amount of labour and activity for the members of a nation and that this is the first and most real wealth, much more than the amount of precious metal which is a mere symbol that rushes to fulfil the demands of industry and hard work, and in spite of any obstacle, flees from inefficiency and idleness. It is equally necessary to know how to apply these maxims to the various situations of a province, to the various circumstances of the population, the climate, the natural or cultivated fertility of the land, to the characteristics of the surroundings, to the needs of neighbouring peoples, and to the differing nature of the products and crafts on which they depend.

Along with all these considerations, we must never lose sight of the universal characteristics of human nature, which is something better regulated by obstacles than by prohibitions. It is characteristic of human beings to throw themselves blindly into their present and immediate concerns, neglecting the future; they love variety and change, albeit only within familiar surroundings, which exercise a stronger influence than any reasoning; they wish to do much, but with the least possible effort; they are stimulated and regulated by certainty, as much of good as of evil, and are disheartened by arbitrariness and uncertainty.

These and other luminous and great principles, assiduously and accurately adapted to the particular circumstances of every state, need to be impressed on the pliant minds of the young. In this way, they will become imbued with that spirit of agile, far-reaching analysis and comparison by which the truth is discovered in all its complexity, and by which alone the science of legislation can be perfected.

With these ends in view, public economy will illuminate the twisted and obscure byways of private jurisprudence. By its aid those who judge or deal with citizens' affairs, which are often closely bound up with the affairs of public bodies, will be able to leave behind the fallible and unreliable rules of private equity and, when interpreting difficult cases, guide themselves instead by the invariable law of utility and the eternal norms of universal equity, which are all firmly grounded on the maxims of public economy.

Moreover, whoever restricts himself within the confines of his science and ignores similar and neighbouring sciences will never become great and famous in his own. An immense network links all truths, and they are more varying, uncertain and confused the more cramped and limited they are; becoming simpler, grander and more dependable only as they expand into a wider space and raise themselves to a higher point of view.

As evidence of these truths, it is enough to recall the times and places when all the sciences were buried in silence in the midst of feudal anarchy and the uproar of arms, so that private jurisprudence became the public legislator. What were the effects? The free internal circulation of merchandise was obstructed; the prompt and speedy transactions of trade were hampered by slow and inflexible procedures; it was thought that the state could be made wealthy by cutting down the expenses of rich individuals with puritanical sumptuary laws, thereby drying up the springs of industry, blunting the stimulus to work and numbing the hope of a better condition which is the vital spark of every body politic; a rigid, near-monastic discipline was imposed on artisanal organisations, forcing them into rival and quarrelling factions which imposed taxes on each other, which set up regulations among themselves, paralysing the development of crafts which feed on freedom and lack of constraint. The field was left free for the tendency (perhaps respectable in its motivations but distinctly unhealthy in its inevitable consequences) to establish a practice inimical to political development: *Let idleness be supported at the public cost, and receive the reward which is owing to effort and graft.* These and others are the effects of restricting jurisprudence within the boundaries of private justice when it ought to embrace all the greatest principles of morals and politics.

Furthermore, the sciences of public economy cannot but increase and ennoble the private aims of the domestic economy, by suggesting means to unite the individual's own utility with that of the public. As we get used to thinking about social affairs and reconsider our ideas about the universal good, the natural love we bear for our own reasoning and the objects which excite in us so many intellectual pleasures, rekindles our enfeebled sense of patriotism.

We no longer think of ourselves as isolated parts, but as the children of society, of the laws and of the Sovereign. The sphere within which our feelings move becomes wider and more lively; selfish passions diminish; social affections spread and are strengthened by the power of the imagination and of habit, and, as we learn to see things as they really are, we distance ourselves from all baseness and cowardice, which are vices arising from a false assessment of things.

In this way, by comparing the various professions of men we gradually come to the amazing and moving realisation that they are all bound together by a chain of reciprocal service, with the result that we come to respect and value them not for their pomp and ostentation, but for their utility and the difficulties which they overcome. We learn just how much respect is due, on the one hand, to the proud indolence of those who lie in rags among the tattered images of their ancestors and, on the other, to the hard-working and wholesome industry of the husbandman; and, while admiring the solitary and austere monk, we do not despise the humble family man who divides a loaf earned through sweat among the tender children of the nation.

Lastly, considerable benefit can be derived from the study of a science which is neither confined to an ivory tower nor surrounds itself with objects remote from use in common life, but which is talked about in all circles and meetings and which daily events continually call to be put to use. Hence, it will help us to defend ourselves, with inner conviction and with that quiet, clear light which the proper study of the sciences infuses in us, both from the ancient prejudices handed down to us by local tradition and from the peevishness and discontent which in all times and places never cease to work on the insecurity and docility of the ignorant.

Nevertheless, this science, however necessary and useful, was one of the last to develop within the human spirit, and it has not yet reached that highest pitch of perfection of which it seems capable. All the arts and sciences were born of our needs, whether primary – those which even a solitary man left to himself will necessarily feel – or secondary ones like curiosity, the desire to distinguish oneself, flight from boredom, that evolve once men are joined in society, through a process of reciprocal observation and imitation as it becomes easier to satisfy our basic needs and intellectual activity increases with the gathering together of thinking beings. There has, therefore, always been public economy and commerce among men who are united in any way whatever. At all times there has been the barter of one superfluous thing in exchange for another necessary thing, of actions for things and of actions for actions. This is the root of all trade. At all times men who have come together for any reason have been compelled, in order to maintain their union and achieve its purpose, to cooperate in a certain number of operations for the common good, and to hand over both the direction and the product of such operations to a supreme magistrate. This is the root of all types of finance and of their administration. But these arrangements were guided only by the chaotic and incoherent cares of the moment, by the pressing presence of need and of the momentary and violent fear of harm, and not by a chain of reasoning and of orderly deductions of one truth from another in the light of the overall needs of society.

Many centuries and an unending series of events and experiences were needed for men to grope their way towards the sciences of economics and to produce that quantity of small circumstances which were to lead some bold and happy genius to bring light into such matters in the face of the resistance put up by private interests and the fantastic illusions of prejudice and error. Indeed, if we turn our eyes to the earliest times, we see that men were scarcer on the face of the Earth in comparison with the present population, but that they had multiplied beyond the resources which nature spontaneously offered to supply their needs; that they were hemmed in by rivers which they did not dare to cross; that they were contained by mountains which they found impassable; that they hardly traded in the goods most necessary to life, instead tearing them from each other's hands by force of arms. The first, because easiest and most necessary, profession among men was hunting. Its continued practice gave them knowledge of grazing animals, and they became shepherds. In this more idle and tranquil state, the spirit of observation began to grow, as did commerce and the stimuli to commerce as men eased themselves into a softer and less rude and fierce lifestyle. Nevertheless, with the growth of needs and of the population, there was call to subjoin art to the spontaneous productions of nature, and men became farmers. But the discovery of metals was the cause of a new revolution in human affairs and raised humanity to a higher level of activity and, as a result, of perfection.

The need for durable metals as materials for the arts, the desire of mortals to distinguish themselves with a monument of industry and power, and their anxious wish to offer to the gods what was dearest and most useful to them, made men both seek for and value the various metals according to how hard they were to find and rare they were. Once a means had been found to divide metal into convenient parts and impose a uniform appearance upon it, these metals gradually became the means of exchange for all types of goods and, hence, the universal representative of them, just as, perhaps, before they were discovered, the most necessary and useful products had been. Such was the origin of money, which was the vehicle whereby the political machine became more mobile and smooth-running. Finally, the harsh environment of men living along the sea coasts forced them to venture on to the high seas thereby increasing communications, movement and the reciprocal exchange of goods and of the luxuries of life.

In the period of which we have some record, Asia was the first commercial market. The fame of the Phoenician voyages can still be heard among us today. With tireless industry, these dauntless sailors procured from the East, from Africa and from Europe all the gifts of nature which were denied to their own small and arid homeland. They exchanged them and spread them where they were lacking, and, with their numberless cargoes, they subjected to tribute the nations which remained cowering in their own lands, competing and warring among themselves.

At a time better known to us, Carthage, the Phoenicians' colony on the Mediterranean, grew up on the ruins of Tyre and Sidon. It embraced the east coast of Africa through the Red Sea and the ports of Eloth and Ezion-Geber,[4] becoming the distributor of gold and the most precious perfumes; sending her fleets to the western coasts and into the Mediterranean; taking wool, iron, cotton, gold and silver from Spain; and even reaching the Cassiritides,[5] now part of Britain, to get tin. In the meantime, Greece flourished as a result of her liberties and the most sublime discoveries of human

---

[4] Modern Aila and Taba respectively.
[5] Now known as the Scilly Isles.

genius. But split into jealous and continually divided republics; except when union was necessary to defend their independence against the barbarians, commerce took second place to democratic strife and Spartan and arrogantly austere military habits.

The Phoceans, a colony of Athens, founded Marseilles – the standing rival of Carthage while Rome was emerging from obscure origins. But once Rome had emerged ambitious and conquering; she profited from alliances with the republics which rivalled Carthage in order to destroy her; and, once Carthage was destroyed, Rome slowly turned her allies into subjects and tributaries. This is a policy which she maintained at all times.

Before this time, Alexander had founded a new empire. Isolated Egypt and ancient India were opened up by his conquering genius, and the seas of the latter felt the weight of foreign fleets. Alexandria was founded and became the second market-place of the two trades, from East and West. Such riches lasted until the reign of the Ptolemies.[6] But in the end, Rome's armies triumphed over all the glories of ancient industry, swallowed all the wealth, and the immense tribute from so many provinces made up the only public economy of the Roman Empire. Constantine's removal of the imperial seat to Byzantium[7] was a turning-point of the greatest consequence. It established on the Hellespont a thriving centre of political and economic business. Surrounded by barbarian and wretched peoples, that stimulus which arises from the emulation of powerful neighbours was now lost. The immense bulwark of the empire, the majesty of a conquering race, and the influx of tributes from all over the world had silenced the imperious voice of need at its centre. But poverty and slavery rekindled desperation and courage in every heart. The Empire of the West collapsed entirely, mown down and torn apart by northern peoples. All the crafts and every kind of industry remained buried. Only in Italy were navigation and trade preserved by the active and restless character of the people. The old republican spirit lay hidden under the ashes of the Roman Empire. Little by little Italy broke part of the chains which had been imposed on her by a fierce but ignorant people. Venetian liberty and industry arose from the swamps of

[6] I.e., until 48–47 BC.
[7] From AD 330.

the Adriatic; Genoa, Pisa and Florence fought among themselves, but against all Europe held dominion of the seas and the lead in manufacturing. The Italian fleets were alone in conducting trade with the Levant through Alexandria, and all the nations of Europe sent all their raw materials to Italy, which was alone in knowing how to work them. Meanwhile, those other nations, in which all administrative activity was broken and torn by feudal government, groaned under a despotism which was all the more devastating for being weak and divided. The Italians' voyages to the north made Flanders into a centre of trade. The example they saw at home awoke the Flemings and made them into the second manufacturers of Europe. The concessions made to tradesmen by the counts of Flanders encouraged the nation, and when they were rescinded they depressed it.[8] Other nations profited by their imprudence, and, as a result, England, France, Holland and Germany, in the shape of the Hanseatic League,[9] came to partake of the wealth and industry which had hitherto belonged solely to the genius of the Italians.

Persecuted everywhere in turn, not so much from misguided zeal as from greed for their wealth, the Jews resorted to the invention of bills of exchange in order to protect their wealth from tyrannical searches. This was a fundamental turning-point for commerce as a result of which communication between trading peoples was made faster, safer and, therefore, greater. The compass was discovered which guided the Portuguese to Africa, where they built up large establishments. Bartholemew Diaz rounded the Cape of Good Hope,[10] an event fatal to Italy, which lost the better part of her trade with the East, that is to say, with India. Soon thereafter,[11] Christopher Columbus, one of those eager spirits whom more commonplace souls, in their timidity and caution, call chimerical or romantic, opened up for Spain a new world, the fruit of his long-standing and long-mocked resolve. The gold that abounded there made the Spaniards greedy enough to lose the love of life,

[8] The period of increased taxation for Flanders can be dated to the beginning of its absorption into Burgundy in 1384.
[9] The Hanseatic League was a cartel of German trading cities. It had begun to secure privileges in Flanders in 1252 and by 1358 was powerful enough to wage and win economic war in their defence.
[10] In 1488.
[11] In 1492.

which had been poisoned at its very roots, and courageous enough to face the dangers of the immense and daunting sea. Rivers of blood flowed and millions of victims were sacrificed apparently to the religion of a God of peace, but really to the voracity for the metal which was the symbol of all pleasures. The easy but cruel conquest of gold made its first owners negligent of crafts and of industry, while the gold itself, following the infallible law of its attraction to the industry and effort which had been set on foot among the nations which were still kept out of America, did not fail to pass from the idle hands of the Spaniards and to circulate in Holland, England and France. Necessity and desperation created freedom and industry in the United Provinces; some merchants became sovereigns of vast kingdoms in the East Indies and the monopoly of trade in spices secured for the nation an inexhaustible supply of wealth. In England, Elizabeth and the wisdom of her Parliaments consolidated English manufacturing superiority and domination of the seas. On the one hand, the famous Navigation Act offered encouragement,[12] and on the other, commercial companies on the Dutch model united the powers of the nation and revived the ancient example of the conquering merchants of Carthage. Louis XIV and Colbert raised up France, invigorating every type of industry and all the fine arts almost at a stroke; the arts of luxury and of peace were wonderfully nourished and encouraged in the midst of ambitious enterprises of conquest; but the fatal act of the Revocation of the Edict of Nantes at a single blow gave to France's competing powers a large portion of her strength and resources.[13]

With the overthrow of the dark idol of peripatetic superstition, the light of the most useful sciences to humanity began to shine in Europe. The keen observational spirit of natural science spread to public economy and to commerce. Bacon had already sown the first seeds of these sciences in England, and they were subsequently developed and brought to fruition by other worthy men of that

---

[12] A reference to a law of 1651 designed to prevent imports into Britain being carried in Dutch ships.
[13] The Edict of Nantes of 1598 granted a measure of religious freedom to non-Catholics in France. Its revocation in 1685 provoked large-scale emigration by the Protestant Huguenots, who accounted for a major section of the artisan and merchant classes.

great nation. The first to make the unknown language of economic reason heard in France was the Marshal de Vauban, who shared the profession of arms with Xenophon, from whom we have received the only monument the ancients left us in this area of politics. Melon, the immortal Montesquieu, Ustariz, Ulloa, the philosopher Hume and the founder in Italy of public economy, abbot Genovesi, as well as many others, have pressed on with this science, from which nothing is missing but the final, though by no means less difficult, touches to make it complete and a sound and widely used practical instrument.

If we turn our attention from distant affairs to our own province, we shall see how far it has fallen from its previously flourishing state, as a result not only of the blaze of war which so often passed across it, but also because of the unequal apportionment of taxes and the multiplication and confusion of the administrations. But our province has been invigorated and lifted to a new and happy order of things under the immortal reign of Maria Theresa, with laws and ordinances which are as simple as they are universal, that have put the means of restoring industry and public happiness into the hands of the legislating prince, removing the destructive element of arbitrariness. But the shortness of the time available and the degree of detail needed to deal not only with our own affairs but also with so many august benefactions, forces me to reserve so happy a theme for my lectures.

It remains for me solemnly to promise that, in setting out the most certain principles concerning agriculture, trade, manufacture, internal policing, and finance, I shall never forget the sacred duty of those responsible for public instruction of always speaking the truth clearly, simply and vigorously. By tracing the primitive origins of things, where they are less entangled by many other relations and variations, we shall be able to uncover precise and non-arbitrary definitions. We shall bring forth the warrant for what we say by breaking complex notions down into their elements and by giving an orderly deduction from the simplest propositions to the most general and complicated truths. At the same time, by continually applying economic principles to our own circumstances I shall try to steer clear of all sterile and abstract speculation and from that sort of impressive apparatus of scientific terminology which makes all the sciences seem mysterious and inaccessible. And I shall avoid magisterial and dogmatic assertions, under whose yoke the initial enthusiasm of the mind is slowed down to a servile imitation and the sciences become a question of the skilful piecing together of agreed terminology.

I am unsure of myself, and the importance of a science which concerns itself with the interests of whole nations daunts me. But I look for encouragement and help from the illustrious youth of Milan. Their compliant intelligence, their heartfelt and untiring spirit and their lively curiosity will help to keep me from falling into the cunning pitfalls of error, to beat back barbarous prejudices and preconceived opinions that might come forth to do battle with the gifts of nature and even, however vainly, with the glorious provisions of our government, to the detriment of the timid and elusive truth. I shall think myself lucky if my diligent efforts contribute to increasing the number of our august Sovereign's enlightened subjects, of true citizens of the fatherland, of virtuous men of sound understanding who give value to human society.

Reflections on the Barbarousness and the Civilisation of Nations and on the Savage State of Man

For a nation to be barbarous, if we understand the term in a precise, philosophical sense, is simply for it to be ignorant of the things that are useful to it and of how to attain them by the readiest means and those most conducive to the happiness of each individual. For a nation to be civilised is for it to be acquainted with these things. The ruler and governor is required to know what is advantageous to his people and how to secure it for them, and to have a desire so to do. The people are required simply not to obstruct by their opinions or habits the true benefits they are offered nor the true means employed to render them happy.

A nation ought not to be called barbarous so long as knowledge and opinion keep pace with each individual's needs and greatest expectations of happiness. But it can be more or less savage, a term which expresses the greater or lesser distance from the highest state of unison achievable among men, and from the greatest possible happiness divided among the greatest number. I keep stopping to provide definitions, but this is the only way we can hope to turn a wayward, unstable science into a more precise and reliable one, and to convert what has been a pretext for the unscrupulous and a formula for blood and misery into a science which is the friend of the people and the guardian of humankind.

A nation can be savage and barbarous; it can be savage without being barbarous; and it can be highly barbarous and highly social at the same time.

When men are joined together by a very few but powerful needs, and when the means to satisfy those needs are out of proportion to the number of the needy, then men will avail themselves of the means which are readiest to hand but which are not the most conducive to the happiness of each individual. In this way, savagery is born from the womb of sensibility and ignorance; so that, in a region which is barren by nature of plants and animals, men will become cannibals, which is the readiest means and, at the same time, the most dangerous for each individual. We have already noted the second possibility. The third comes about when men are held together by many needs, and when many misguided means are employed to secure some of them and there is much ignorance about how to supply the rest. This last is the most widespread situation, the most productive of different permutations, and the one of closest interest to us. We must examine how man comes to make mistakes, by what secret and fateful chain of events, he comes to leap from simple and reliable sensations clean over the truth into the infinite abyss of error, and how much falsehood he has to pass through to return to the truth.

The fewer ideas a man has and the fewer comparisons he makes, the more imperious and unshakeable the needs that arise in him. The readiest means which presents itself to the mind is preferred to the most effective, and the most effective, even if it is perhaps more dangerous, is preferred to the less effective as long as the danger is either unknown or only distantly and obscurely perceptible. But, what is more, men reason on the basis of their own feelings, and the strongest and most lasting impressions are those to which we give the most weight, in keeping with that general impulse, that force of gravity, that natural bent by which sensible beings draw in new impressions and unite them with old, existing ones.

Diffidence is always proportional to the number of adverse experiences which either are known about in others or have been undergone at first hand, the latter being much more powerful than the former. But the similarities which man finds are not those which are made by Nature who, set upon an inaccessible throne, stamps her energy on every being and produces from a single phenomenon an infinite variety of others which are modified by the circumstances and organisation of each sentient creature. The fewer preconceived models a man has with which to compare the new feelings which arise in him, the more willing he will be to make changes. Thus, savages are quick, enterprising and utterly confident about the means they adopt to satisfy their wants. But, at the same time, they are hesitant and easily manipulated when confronted by new and unfamiliar things, because they seem much newer and more unfamiliar to them than they do to civilised men. Civilised men, by contrast, are slow and diffident in all matters because they have many needs to coordinate and to balance; they are slow to make changes because, among the many ideas and possibilities they revolve, they always find some tried and tested model which seems good to them and which saves them the trouble of thinking – something they will only have recourse to when forced into it by necessity and a sense of want.

Uniformity of habits among savages is purely negative, because it lasts only until there arises some occasion to depart from it. But uniformity is positive among civilised men, because it arises from diffidence and foresight. Thus, the barbarousness of the savage is restricted to a single set of ideas, whereas that of the civilised man is more contagious and universal. Savages may sometimes act barbarously, but the civilised reason barbarously. The passions of the former taken as a whole are powerful, but they are disconnected, with repeated episodes of effort and of rest, of violence and of calm. But in the latter, the passions are generally divided up into small parcels which are methodically linked together, one dwindling as the other grows stronger, in minute, imperceptible stages. In this way, civilised peoples come close to the savage state with respect to the strongest passions and savages approach the customs of civilised peoples in their superstitions, which are their form of civilisation. Anyone can see that every savage has some sort of civilisation, that every civilised man has some savage side to him, and that these two states are closely bound up with each other and impossible to separate.

All the feelings a man has, whatever state he is in, are always natural to him. Man in a state of savagery does not differ from man in a state of society with respect to their physical strength and their relation to the things and people around them alone, there is also an habitual difference in his feelings. Man entered into the state of society from the state of savagery precisely because his natural feelings had changed. As a result, the natural feelings of the savage do not provide the norm of the original public law.

But nor can the natural feelings with which man entered into society be a guide to the present public law, because the original state of society has itself changed, and it is in the very nature of sociability to change.

The laws of savages are the sum of the combination of their passions. The laws of civilised nations are, when just, the result of the difference of those same passions, which make up the common reason.

Every nation has its religion, its customs and its laws. Every religion boils down either to monotheism or to polytheism; every custom is either Stoic or Epicurean; and every system of laws reduces either to a law of interpretation and equity or to rigid and literal law. The various permutations of these six elements, three of which exist in every nation, determine the multifarious characters which distinguish one nation from another.

This century has seen a debate on whether man is happier in the savage or the social state. Men in the former state are represented as naked and wandering, but girded with strength and vigour; neither timid nor ferocious; facing up to the few evils nature presents them armed with the courage of their ignorance, the hardiness of their constitution and their blithe lack of foresight. They are represented as enjoying a state of somnolence or indolence rather than the boredom that oppresses or goads civilised men: uncaring of death, of which they know nothing, and wrapped up in their most immediate sensations, they are affected by passions directed at things, not by passions directed at the means for obtaining them (passions these last, that increase as the passions for things decline). And so they merge blissfully into the bosom of matter without having cursed their existence. The earth is rarely bathed in human blood; and then only in brief combats between individuals armed simply with the weapons nature provides; and the sequence of events in those obscure but happy generations is not a long and calculated bloodbath, nor an uninterrupted tradition of glorious crimes that allow each century to draw on the precedent of the last to justify its sacrificing poor trembling mortals to a few bold and crafty ones. This is the picture some melancholy philosophers draw of the savage state;[1] so their listeners,

[1] Beccaria here refers to J. J. Rousseau's *Discourse on the Origin and Foundation of Inequality* (1755).

finding themselves so far from happiness themselves, plunge into a state of desperation and insensibility, and find their way back to the wild in their minds and imaginations, since they cannot or do not wish to do so in reality. And in this way they close off all those routes through which individual sensibilities communicate with each other; fierce emotions arise in their desiccated hearts which lead them to deny others' sentient existence and to imagine themselves the only beings in the universe and act accordingly. It is true that the consequences of a principle, however fatal, do not destroy it as internal contradictions do. But they do have the effect of obliging us to retrace the steps back to the principle itself, in the suspicion that it may be false. So the older we imagine the universe to be, and the more varied the physical and moral revolutions we imagine it to have undergone, the more likely it seems that the original principle was false and destructive, since its effects did not last. So let us analyse this savage state, taking into consideration not only whether it was happy (for here the misanthropes may be right), but its viability and durability.

In the present century there has been discussion of whether man is happier in the savage state or in the social state.

Let us imagine we have before us all the animals in the world. Which will be the species that will join together in society, to experience all goods and evils, to become the conqueror of nature and the disturber of the universe? Those fierce and shaggy beasts which we see armed with fearful fangs, in addition to being restricted to hot climes and being short-lived and, for that reason, with their more momentary needs, less observant, must be held back from perfecting themselves by the natural perfection of some of their organs and the lack or dullness of others; and since there exists this imbalance in their faculties, all of them will be directed to the operation of the more perfect organs. If an animal is to perfect itself and improve its condition, its needs must be various and distributed across all its faculties; needing and lacking everything, it must have adaptable organs and, at the same time, it must experience enough resistance from the objects surrounding it to necessitate a constant, varied experimentation on its part. In addition, there must be a certain proportion between the size of the organs put to work and the objects worked on.

Now, the human animal has organs adapted to an easy approach to and withdrawal from a great number of objects which are suited to his needs and which, by resisting his attempts to mould them, excite and develop his industriousness. All his senses are in themselves less perfect than those of other animals; but they are balanced in such a way that none is dominant over the others, whereas if one sense is too conspicuous, it has the same effect in a sensitive being as too great inequality of goods has in political bodies.

There will be greater reciprocity in the association of ideas in man, therefore; and, since the basic configurations of ideas are less fixed, more complex combinations will become possible, incorporating a greater number of elements.

In this state, the dangers of wild animals soon teach various individuals to come together. Nature set limits to the spread of humankind and offered human beings incentives to come together with the phenomena of the heavens and of the earth, which was perhaps not fully peopled and not settled in its orbit, with the physical position of rivers, untraversable by unskilled savages, with inhospitable chains of mountains and with the as yet unconquered sea.

The formation of hunting parties encouraged the invention of weapons and stratagems to use against wild animals, but which, as a disproportion developed between needs and the means for satisfying them, later became the instruments for men's destroying their own kind. The closer men are to primary sensations, and the more they are ruled by their primitive passions, and the morality of their actions is measured in terms of natural forces and the vigour of their souls, the less the differences between them diminish and their feelings and actions come to resemble each other. This can be clearly seen even in a state of society: violent passions bring all ranks and creeds down to the same level; they unite the extremes; and they make all men either brothers or competitors, because an extreme passion, which is nothing but the concentration of all the soul's strength on a single object, leaves the whole range of adjunct feelings inoperative and unused.

It was a case of the strong fighting the strong, therefore. But it was precisely because of this balance of power that the industry of warfare developed, that social conventions were established and new discoveries were made. The arts and sciences thus grew in proportion to need, always with the smallest possible progress in the given circumstances, for the law of least action applies no less rigorously in morals than it does in physics.

What, then, could prevent the inexorable force of necessity from bringing about human sociability? The impossibility of our ever returning to one of the extremes of our nature, makes it the more imperative that we should progress as rapidly and smoothly as possible towards the other, that is to say, to the highest civilisation.

Moreover, those who say that a rare equality was the happy attribute of the first societies do not tell the whole story. For those who were the first to escape from a disorderly and sterile nature rushed to occupy all the few fertile and secure places, and they had to enslave the others who were slower to take refuge and who accepted all the iniquitous terms of the first inhabitants rather than face an inevitable death. Dense and invincible ignorance helped to perpetuate the rule of fear and slavery, which is the first and last state through which nations pass that simply respond to immediate evils rather than being guided by foresight, something which can only be learnt by experience of the very evils which ought to be avoided.

Just as the natural philosopher sees the current order of things on the face of the globe, but can also read in its innards the traces of the past disorders that created it and whose effects are still discernible in nature, so the moralist, observing the advantages of our current state and the progress that has been made in the science of happiness, can perceive them as the outcome of ancient disorders; and he may dare to predict that current evils are just the inevitable tremors and upheavals arising from that process, after which the nations will march on towards a final, still very distant, state of equality and happiness.

Reflections on Manners and Customs

Whenever a nation changes its customs and manners it does so either out of necessity, out of boredom or because of a shock. By customs, I mean the results of the emotions and passions which move men; by manners, I mean their external behaviour, that is to say, that language of action which every society possesses to allow men to exploit these same results and show them off to their best advantage.

Necessity alters customs more than manners; and boredom alters manners more than customs; shock affects both equally. The changes brought about by necessity are rarer but more stubborn and durable; those brought about by boredom are more frequent but less lasting; those resulting from shock may be either durable or short-lived, rare or frequent, according to whether they are inspired by deep-rooted natural feelings or artificial sentiments.

Necessity has a greater influence on customs than on manners, because the former derive from the succession of human needs and the latter from the succession of opinions; and needs command whilst opinions advise. Opinions gain their ascendancy as a result of mental laziness: we are much happier sticking with the falsehoods we know than exploring new truths, and we allow ourselves to be beguiled by the ease with which something can be imagined or done, without assessing the clarity of our imaginings or the usefulness of our deeds. But the influence of manners and of opinions on the affections and the customs of men is such that necessity does not produce the full change which it would if it acted unimpeded on man. Because we are attached to the current state of our ideas, whose ease of use we appreciate, we try to preserve existing manners and integrate them with new customs, however pointless or incompatible they may be.

Political necessities are in inverse proportion to the means which nature offers and in direct proportion to the number of men who make up society. Hence, they diminish with the spontaneous aid of the soil and grow with manufactured products. For this reason, among the nations of antiquity, as among those in rich and fertile regions, changes are in this respect fewer than those in modern nations.

But boredom, which arises out of the smaller quantity of sensations which long-established manners offer compared with when they were new, slowly transforms those very manners, albeit always following the law of graduated uniformity which applies as much in morals as in physics. People want novely without effort, they change their practice while holding on to their opinion and vice versa. Private manners change more easily than public ones; those which concern matters of indifference, more than those which concern matters of importance.

The amount of attention we dedicate to any given undertaking depends on two factors: its importance and its difficulty. The less closely it touches on our own personal interests, the greater the influence the factor of difficulty will come to assume.

When many different individuals with conflicting interests are involved in the affair, the perspectives being brought to bear on the subject will differ so greatly that the only way to reach an agreement will be to fall back on the old and trusted ways. Hence, in a nation which is governed by many individuals with disunited interests, vices and disorder have become so time-hallowed, so deeply rooted, so much a part of the system, that they have taken on the semblance of virtue and orderliness. Necessity would rectify them if men did not confuse the needs of their own particular class with those of society as a whole, and if they took account not only of violent and momentary evils but also of those which grow slowly and by imperceptible degrees diverge from the ancient but temporary good from which they arose.

But boredom is too particular and private a feeling to have a place in public affairs, except perhaps in a despotism where the public interest is a private interest. Moreover, boredom presupposes an already enlightened nation, and has no power over savages to make them change their ways. It is better adapted to improve civilised nations than to hold back those which are already corrupt. It can certainly speed up the dissemination of things and feelings, once they have already been introduced, but it is not enough to motivate major changes, which can only be brought about by the stronger compulsions of necessity or shock. Shock is experienced by one on the receiving end as a passion caused by an alien and powerful impression which has little or no connection with the ideas already in his mind. Keeping him separated from other factors, it directs him towards what it presents to him. For its perpetrator, shock consists of a novel, vigorous and decisive action. Men are shocked by conquests, by new religions and sets of laws, by terror and by outstanding generosity. Some of these shocks are stable, others transitory; some start in the realm of opinion and are translated into reality, while others move in the opposite direction.

Some manners are public and others are private. Men are attached to the former by veneration, because of the importance of the interests they involve and because the common people tend to confuse what is incidental with what is essential, words with things, and means with ends, while those who are concerned with public affairs are incorrigibly infatuated with the status quo. Men are attached to private manners by fond habit and by easy and contagious imitation.

Likewise, there are public customs and private customs. Among public customs are the spirit of common morality and traditional prudence as well as the different tactics which public men employ when dealing with the sovereign and with subjects. These last are praised by men of today and by the common people because they were praised in the past and by great men, and perhaps because praise tends to be more spontaneous when the person praised and the person doing the praising are close in rank. Faced with things they would be incapable of doing, or do not have the power to do, people react with admiration or hatred; their sincerer admiration is reserved for things that it would lie within their power to do in similar circumstances. Private customs are those which are operative when men are dealing with their private affairs and pleasures, when they know each other better, because the spirit is less constrained when it comes to amusements.

On the whole private customs guide public customs. Though the public good requires a higher aim, men carry over to it their domestic ideas and their timorous family worries. Should those who have always been accustomed to abasing themselves use the hands they have sullied by wielding petty school-masterly whips to write down the decrees of public happiness?

The legislator can more easily change public manners than public customs, but conversely he can more easily change private customs than public manners. For the sovereign will find as many secret opponents of change in public customs as there are magistrates. Since private customs are connected with interests and manners with pastimes and entertainments, the former can be changed by re-directing interests, and the latter can only be corrected slowly and by indirect means. But it is not in the interests of those who administer public affairs to see any change in public manners, because if the status quo is maintained, magistrates are able to satisfy their private interests, while appeasing and conciliating public opinion.

The firmness with which opinions are rooted in the human mind depends not on their plausibility, but on their importance. They give to and receive from manners a force and energy which limits the power of the supreme authority itself, constraining it to combat that force by indirect means.

Abstract opinions are more likely to be sustained by manners than to be sustainers of them. Manners which arise from passions with clear and well-defined objects are constant. Those which do not, if left to themselves, tend to change of their own accord, so that an object which at present inspires the greatest consensus will in future become the source of the greatest discord.

Men change their passions and feelings more than their habits, because the present acts more strongly on inner movements and the past on outer ones.

Manners influence customs by reason of their multiplicity, their long standing, their variety and the nature of the impression they produce.

So far as the multiplicity of manners is concerned, the fact that a whole set of manners tends to proliferate around a single custom certainly contributes to the tenacity with which men cling to that custom, but it reduces its real effectiveness. For although it is true that incidental things do sustain the essential things around which they gravitate and on which they depend, they also tend to divide and dissipate attention and thus to undermine the unity of feeling which alone is able to produce great and fateful things.

The multiplicity of manners, by increasing men's sensations and occupations, reduces the power of the passions, and softens fierce peoples, but weakens those which are already soft. It increases the spirit of outward sociability, which brings bodies together but sets minds asunder. Because important interests, for which it is worth making some sacrifice for the sake of unity, bring men together; but small interests, which are annulled when they lapse, divide them. Since conventions are but means to obtain the pleasures of society, when they are multiplied they divide interests into smaller parts and set minds asunder.

When there is a multiplicity of manners, and these manners are frequently repeated over a certain period of time, a spirit of imitation and habit is generated which in turn serves to perpetuate them. This traps men with the invincible force of the senses by means of varied and pleasant entertainments which at once allure and excite them, given that they are attracted by what nourishes strong reasons for hope and fear. The importance of the reasons disguises the puerile frivolity of the manners themselves, which often give importance to things which do not deserve it. In this way they burden the means which lead to given ends with a whole baggage of excess sentiments, making people sluggish, if persistent, in their pursuit of those ends. And this gives rise to that dilatory prudence which stands by as the fleet and fortunate course of human actions is brought to a standstill by the obstacles in its path.

The multiplicity of manners accustoms men to particularise everything because they generally confuse signs with things. Both the most ignorant and the wisest tend to see particulars from a single point of view; the former do so because they do not see distinctions; and the latter because they see the connections among things. The former derive many facts from one; and the latter derive only one from many. Therefore, numerous practices produce different norms of the good and the bad, and reduce the actions which are concerned with society to neighbouring but unequal portions, which do not tend to fixed points. All the same, in society the disarray of individual interests ought to be offset in terms of the general interest, so as not to upset the common progress.

Among the common people, age has always been a motive for unreasoning veneration. This is both out of distaste for the things of the present – the only ones, it appears, to give offence – and also because, faced with the choice between veneration, on the one hand, and a long and laborious investigation of the truth, on the other, most of them would have little hesitation in choosing the former, given their natural inclination to avoid mental effort except where it is unavoidable. Hence common people look only to the immediately striking realities of the present to find the causes of current evils, although many modern disorders may be the effects of a single disorder in the past.

Variation in the underlying laws, the usurpation of one part over the whole, is perfectly consistent with immobility in practices and with a sacred and earnest austerity in conserving them. Common people confuse practices with laws, and names, titles, uniforms and the temporary rules of specific groups with the foundations of public well-being, with the expression of the general will which arises from the balancing of opposed interests and the cooperation of those who are joined together. Manners are simpler than the laws, just as language is much simpler than the ideas it conveys, and the multiplicity of the former distracts men's attention from the latter; and they serve cunning tyranny as so many thick veils behind which safely to hide its usurpations. By putting a little good on show, men have always been able to hide much evil; strength can then find its justifications and blame everything on weakness. It is for this reason that corrupt courts, for all their arbitrary decisions, are extremely strict in enforcing the formalities of justice, so much so that in governments which have already foundered even good contributes to their ruin, because it fuels or retards the development of that popular mistrust which is the precursor of revolution.

A great difference between public and private practices makes the former more respected. Common people reckon moral phenomena as they do physical phenomena, and they do not consider the distinctions in the former sort except in terms of the different sensations which accompany them. In this way, from the officially sanctioned singularity of a man's garb, it is normal to infer the singularity of the man. So, practices originally associated with objects of respect or contempt can, if applied to other, more indifferent matters, communicate to them those earlier feelings of respect or contempt.

New manners which derive from opinions begin with fanaticism and mystery, are spread by imposture and veneration, and continue as habit and spectacle, subsequently becoming objects of ornament and pleasure, and ending up as the butt of ridicule and ignominy.

New manners tend to imitate the old with slight variations, especially when fanaticism and mystery loom large. For man tries to change the order of his ideas without changing his habits, and prefers to introduce new interpretations of and new ends for old practices rather than manners which are wholly new and different. It is for this reason that there is greater resistance to opinions which change habits than to those which are consistent with the old ways.

Only rarely have manners arisen by being instituted or by spontaneous convention. For the most part, they have grown up under the pressure of various necessities – even though when this pressure ceases to be felt, with the passage of time, the resulting manners remain in place through sheer force of habit aided by the efforts of the scoundrels who benefit from them, who attempt to pull the wool over people's eyes by dwelling on the array of meanings they have acquired while glossing over their frivolous origins and the now irrelevant necessity that produced them.

Allegories and allusions are not the offspring of enthusiasm and vehement passions; they condense the feelings, rather than expanding them; they simplify objects instead of complicating them. Therefore, new sects which break away from the old never begin by adding, rather they subtract. Sudden revolutions which come about from strong passions are destructive; only those which are conducted gradually, by reflection and lesser passions, that is by feelings, are constructive.

Some manners impose veneration and respect, others fear and abasement, others again misery and suffering, and yet others joy and celebration.

The first sort hold you back by interposing a sensible distance between you and their object, which they hide in a swarming crowd of incidental elements so as to prevent comparisons and the scrutiny from both of which contempt arises. The mass of things blocks up our imagination just as their elements do our reason. These manners place a necessary brake on men, who aim always at equality in order to secure their own superiority, but in doing so, they do not necessarily go to the other extreme and fill them with a base fear of others' contempt, at least as long as the distance between you and the object is incalculable, and if it seems to be bridgeable, they stimulate a useful spirit of emulation.

The second sort oppress you by requiring you to show all the signs of your dependence and smallness, and by taking away from you everything which encourages you to have confidence in yourselves. For man has perhaps as much need to rule over himself as he does over others. The accompanying sad, terrible and dreary manners condemn you to drink in slow bitter gulps uncertainty, terror and self-contempt, a contempt which is fatal in a free man, who is always bad when abased. Weakened souls perpetuate the evils of the nation because they do not oppose them but evade them; they do not destroy them but try to off-load them on to others. Life becomes something foreign to us: neither the present nor the future belongs to us!, cries the poor wretch in his downtrodden heart, he is one of those threatening earthly deities who damn our present existence and throw uncertainty on our future. Celebratory manners contribute to the happiness of men and therefore to their virtue, or at least to the negative virtues. Because he has lost his sensitivity to others' sufferings, the happy man rarely becomes a scoundrel; even if he is not generous, he has no cause to embark on the restless and obscure path of iniquity. Public pleasures reduce the intensity of the search for private pleasures, which are the most pernicious under the present system. But when a people, of its own accord, sets up public revelries, where crowds flock to stupefy themselves with noise and drunkenness, then you can confidently say: this is an enslaved and unhappy people. Celebratory manners encourage the spirit of brotherhood to which joy and suffering equally prompt us, though with the difference that joy renders our society more universal, while suffering drives us to choose a small number of special friends from whom we demand the paradoxical service of at the same time diverting us from our grief and of empathising with it.

Some associations are based on real interests and others on the needs of opinion. The latter are full of manners and ceremonies which are necessary to call to mind the ideas which bind them together. The very taking part in the ceremonial engages its participants, satisfying their self-esteem with an appearance of public service and command.

All customs depend on opinion. In order to enforce the observance of a custom, the laws themselves must produce an opinion, for the man who is unpersuaded will always reckon on avoiding punishment, a reckoning which cannot be entirely eliminated. Hence, most laws ought to be indirect to inspire customs which are desired and accepted by the subjects – the only stable and just customs, because the only ones that can make men happy, which they do by stimulating and carefully encouraging in men's hearts the sources of morality, which are fear, surprise, compassion, pleasure and order.

Not everything which is useful to the commonwealth ought to be directly ordained, although everything which is harmful ought to banned. Hence, all laws which restrict men's personal freedom must be limited and guided by necessity; and the laws which aim only at positive utility ought not to restrict personal freedom. The proximate and efficient cause of actions is the flight from pain, their final cause is the love of pleasure. Hence, the customs of a nation are determined more by the evils which beset it than by the pleasures which it enjoys or expects.

Man rests in good times and acts when in pain. Hence, a nation's advantages can, at most, determine its negative customs, but its positive customs are determined by its real or feared deficiencies. So, in setting up canons of conduct, man always goes to extremes, and he is more likely to fall into the good by chance, while fleeing from some evil, than to achieve it by design. Fear takes up the whole of his attention and makes it rush to the end of a whole series of ideas connected with what is feared, passing over the middle points.

Climate does not figure as a prominent and immediate cause of the underlying nature of the various nations, but only as a partial and remote factor. Instead we should attend to the fertility or sterility of humankind and of the earth, neither of which is a product of climate alone. And, to forestall objections on this point, we must distinguish the untilled abundance of the soil from its abundance under cultivation.

All societies formed by scattered and savage men, are based on the individual ownership of goods, just as those societies which are formed out of the first sort of society and which are based on the community of belongings. Thus, it may be that in the sterile and freezing North, the republican spirit of freedom and independence of those peoples was the product of respect for things acquired, which were rendered valuable by the effort expended on the miserly soil and by the blood spilt by rivals. Indeed, the authority of the sovereign in those nations was limited by his being accorded tributes only by choice and spontaneously, and, therefore, at each step of the way there was a brake on feudal power (another phenomenon that derived from the preciousness of possessions in these societies). By contrast, the abundance which is more common in southern climates could make those peoples less fiercely and stubbornly acquisitive and more open to fearful ideas of religion and the soft feelings of love, which prevail where other needs are less pressing. Perhaps for this reason, they were more easily subjugated by despotism. Therefore, we find opinion ruling in the South and necessity in the North; in the latter opinions are subordinated to needs, in the former needs obey opinions.

But even in those fertile climes where nature offers the most propitious conditions for human organisation and development, that same nature does not allow men dispensation from the continuous exercise of their faculties. Where urgent bodily needs are easily satisfied, there springs up boredom whose tickling unease pushes men into the inexhaustible infinity of invented pleasures and opinions. Those in power permit the opinions which are useful and suppress those which are useless or opposed to themselves. For this reason, it is the southern peoples who, for the most part, come earliest to knowledge of the arts, to the cultivation of letters and the sciences. But all the other nations can reach them, albeit by different paths.

There are, therefore, two types of perfected society. One is forced into the arms of activity and industriousness by the constant necessity imposed by the sterile soil. In their fullest perfection, these societies arrive at the highest degree of freedom. But, since the peace and tranquillity which result from a long and stable balance of all the powers make nations lose their healthy fear and their unyielding suspicion of change, it is necessary if this freedom is to be preserved, that the society make advances in it which are proportional to and stimulated by losses of it. The perfection of a given moment is not the perfection of the long term. Painful feelings are necessary to men and necessary to nations, a sad but obvious necessity. But the slightest ills necessary to a nation should be so far as possible equally divided, just like the greatest happiness.

The other type of nation is that which develops by means of opinions. Its chief characteristic is stability: it quickly throws itself into the arms of despotism and sleeps there for generations, showing signs of life only when, from time to time, unexpected convulsions make themselves felt. Universal and durable impressions are always the effect of physical events and relations: everything, therefore, is set up in favour of him who first takes control of those fortunate circumstances in which men come together under the influence of physical forces.

Thus, opinion and necessity are the two points from which nations set off in pursuing their perfectability. Fear is the single emotion from which they arise, an emotion present in all constitutions, but which produces different effects in different constitutions.

The wisdom of nations is almost always the fruit of former unhappiness.

The perfection of a given moment is not the perfection of the long term; there must be some way out of the advantages which a nation confers on itself.

The obscurity of physical causes multiplies the effectiveness of moral causes in the eyes of the people.

In despotism, man is below the level of his natural feelings; in republics, he is above it; in monarchies, he is on that level.

Nations pay more attention to perfecting their institutions and send out a brighter light the more corrupt they are.

On Luxury

§31. With the burgeoning of commercial activity, the concentration of land in the hands of a small number of people, the accumulation of capital by a few individuals, and, in short, the inequality of wealth, men developed a new way of utilising that wealth. For a large proportion of humankind drag out their wearisome life and keep their miserable family alive in humble obscurity, without the pangs of envy. Many can live more expansively and enjoy a certain ease and comfort; they can also show off to others and cut a figure with elegance and the trappings of power with which they tacitly intimidate those poorer than themselves and assert their dominance over them. Some few are so rich in the means for obtaining all the comforts and pleasures of life that, having come to the end of their inevitably limited capacity for pleasure and sensation, they are driven by vanity and ostentation to involve others in their power and their means for getting many pleasures. So the rich man's opulent and haughty liberality differs from a genuinely compassionate and discriminating charity only in its motives and in the carelessness with which the former distributes his gifts and throws his money around.

My aim in this description was to convey to you what luxury is, and show more or less what men mean by the word. I say 'more or less' because it is hard to give an exact definition of a term that means very different things to different people depending on their differing circumstances and levels of civilisation. Should we say that luxury is every expense which goes beyond the bare necessities? But what do the bare necessities consist of? Are they the bare minimum necessary for a man to survive, or the bare minimum he needs to live without suffering? But these limits will vary according to the different upbringings men receive and differences in temperament. Should luxury be defined as what enables us to escape pain, or just as what gives us pleasure? But where does pain end and pleasure begin? For many, doing without a pleasure is a great pain. For some people, it would be a source of great misery not to be dripping with gold; for them, dressing in this way would not be a luxury. Should we then say that luxury is every expense that is above a man's station? But have the dividing lines which separate these stations ever been drawn? Can anyone adjudicate that some expenses are proper to the citizen and others to the gentleman?

It would be tiresome and superfluous to set out all the definitions that have been given of the word 'luxury', because some have wanted to use it for one complex notion and others for another. From this variety of opinions there have arisen all the questions about whether luxury is useful or harmful to the political and moral life of the state and whether it contributes to the happiness, or to the misery, of men. Our aim is not to get carried away with such enquiries, but to give an exact account of how luxury is to be understood as an economic phenomenon, and to see what influence the mode of living and spending which men call 'luxury' has on the economy of the state.

To reach a good definition of luxury, we must take from among the many ideas that are associated with this notion only those that are constant. In accordance with this condition, we may take it, therefore, that there are pains to escape which it is necessary to obtain a pleasure, since it is precisely the lack of that pleasure that constitutes the pain being felt. There are also pains which can be relieved by simply removing their cause; but although we feel pleasure in the removal of the pain, once it has been removed, we experience no further pleasure at all. Hunger is a pain of this second type: once I have driven it off by eating some food, I am not left feeling any kind of pleasure; and the pain that arises from hunger does not spring from the fact that I am without one kind of food rather than another, but from an impression which is independent of the nature and state of our ideas. If I have a desire for one kind of food rather than another, and the lack of it upsets me, this is a pain of the first sort, to cure which I can do nothing but search out that food or an equivalent pleasure, or else to suppress my desire for it, as befits a wise and temperate man. For even when a particularly enticing pleasure or material gain is in prospect, what actually prompts us to act is the feeling of restlessness that is produced in us by that pleasure or advantage, as it vividly impresses itself on our senses: a feeling of dissatisfaction that is experienced as a pain like any other.

It is the task of the moral sciences and not of political economy to discuss this truth at length and explore all its implications and examine it from every angle. For present purposes, it is enough to have taken proper note of it, and I hope readers will be convinced if they think back over their own experience, that we only act to avoid a pain; and freedom itself will be found to consist in a man's ability to stir up in himself at will feelings of restlessness opposite to those that might lead him into mischief.

Granted all this, we will define luxury as every expense incurred to rid us of the pains that are privations of pleasure. This definition necessarily extends to the idea of pursuing a pleasure that outlasts the pain which was disturbing us, or, at least, which outlasts our original intention of freeing ourselves from the pain. Someone who is tormented at not having a certain sort of food, is not tormented merely by the desire to get rid of hunger, but by not having that very taste; by contrast, any food which is not disgusting will do for someone who wants merely to satisfy his hunger.

§32. The first thing that follows from this definition is that luxury can be found in all conditions and at all times among sociable men, because at all times and in all conditions men who enjoy the advantages of co-operation and mutual aid are accustomed not merely to satisfying their needs, but to satisfying them pleasantly and comfortably. As men came to realise that they could live the more pleasurably and comfortably the more of their fellows they could induce to procure their pleasures and comfort for them; and as they further realised that this became easier and more frequent the more they succeeded in distinguishing themselves from others and standing out from the crowd, so gradually there arose the need for pleasures, that is, the indeterminate feeling of being deprived that is boredom, and the desire to stand out that is vanity, which make up the two sources of luxury, as can be seen from the definition given. So long as there is society, there will always be boredom and vanity in men because they are inevitable consequences of the relations that arise among those who contract with each other. Therefore there will always be luxury in the broad meaning of the term.

Indeed, anyone who considers the whole of human nature in a broad, universal sense, will find that these same two qualities of mind are deeply rooted even in savages. For their need for pleasures is manifested in the avidity with which they wolf down intoxicating liquors, which are employed by European colonisers to lure them into slavery, in all of their many festivals and war-dances, in all the complicated machinery of the long and solemn ceremonies which they too have (though we might think them so close to simple and unsophisticated nature and so far from our arts and institutions), to mark their funerals and their marriages and in all the turning-points of human life. Where their desire to distinguish themselves is concerned, moreover, there is clear evidence of this if we think about how much gold and how many uncut and rough jewels we have cheated them of in exchange for a few strings of coral and baubles of coloured glass, or if we think about the way in which Africans, who go around half-naked most of the time, still set such great store by and take such pride in some battered hat and a tattered jacket, the wretched cast-off of some European, who bartered it for gold and slaves, which then becomes the ceremonial dress of kings and great men. And the poorest, lacking a great fortune, have to make do with tattooing and searing their flesh in order to stand out from their peers by virtue of the nobility and unfading distinction of their skins.

And anyone who cared to look for luxury among those ancient republics that are so prized for their poverty and frugality would be sure to find it, whatever some might say. In Sparta itself, that same Sparta into which Lycurgus introduced a mixture of military and monastic discipline, there were both the need for pleasure and the desire to stand out. But both were so well integrated into the political constitution that everything contributed to the good of the state, became a public virtue (at least according to the uncritical accounts of ancient historians), whereas all other forms of luxury were considered harmful in that society. The Spartans did get bored, but only with peace and security; they wanted to feel the blows of risk and tumult. The sound of praise was pleasing and sweet to them, all the more so when it issued forth confused and muffled in the midst of the clash of spears and swords, and mingled with the piteous groans of the defeated and captured enemy. I believe that every single one of those sober and severe Spartans smiled proudly to find himself girded with iron and weighed down with arms, and went to great pains to seek out the finest weapons and the most threatening. And their women, who hardened their souls against all the many promptings of nature and instinct, directed their inalienable vanity to cultivating a severity of dress that brought them closer to masculine vigour and force.

From the foregoing it can be seen that to try to root luxury out of a society would be tantamount to trying to destroy one of man's innate faculties. It can also be seen that luxury can be either harmful or useful, according to how well it fits in with or conflicts with (or, to be more precise, how it arises from) the circumstances and the laws of a particular state, which may be good or bad. The pain that arises from the deprivation of pleasures gives rise to love for comforts and to desire for pleasing sensations that flatter and pamper our useless lives. Then it gives rise to the pressing and restless itch to stand out from the crowd and to all the varieties of vanity that serve to bend others to our desires.

We must distinguish two main sorts of luxury or ways of escaping from the pain that derives from being deprived of pleasure. For, on the one hand, I may choose to indulge myself with pleasures and comforts, on the other, I may seek to distinguish myself from the crowd by performing actions that are not in the least productive and have no practical effects, or more generally, do not presuppose the idea of exchange. This sort can be called luxury of action or moral and political luxury; the other sort can be called luxury of contracts or economic luxury.

§33. Each of these types of luxury can be divided into the luxury of comfort and the luxury of ostentation. But, restricting ourselves to economic luxury, we shall divide spending on luxuries into the kind that exchanges goods for goods and the kind that exchanges goods for actions, such as personal services, a large entourage and so forth.

Anyone can see that the kind of spending on luxuries that exchanges goods for goods is much more useful than the kind that exchanges goods for actions, and that the latter may even be harmful inasmuch as the people employed to perform these actions could be employed in producing goods or making goods fit to be used by everyone. But this will only truly harm nations where there is a lack of labour for the fields and industry, a lack which will only occur when the trade in merchandise and manufactures is obstructed, because when the earth is fully cultivated, with industry thriving in open competition, that is to say, both agriculture and industry have achieved the greatest possible freedom, far from reducing the comparative number of luxury contracts of goods for goods, the luxury contracting of goods for actions can take place without causing any harm, since those who receive payment for their actions will exchange it for goods.

From this we can see one of the marvellous effects of the circulation of goods and labour, which operates in such a way that useless actions do not necessarily constitute a loss to society, either in terms of time or products; and this is the more true the vaster and more efficient the network of exchanges. Indeed, the effect of this circulation brings it about that actions that, in other circumstances, might be useless or vicious, produce the excellent effect of competition among the buyers in favour of the sellers of consumable goods so that, by keeping up their prices, the original and unique riches of the land are kept in good standing.

§34. Now, those forms of expenditure, whatever they might be, which exchange goods for goods are more useful to the state if they are made by exchanging the goods of that same country. For, supposing that each of two things exchanged for the other are of equivalent value, both of them will represent effort and food circulating within the state at twice the rate of things exchanged for foreign goods; for in the case of foreign goods, half of the labour and food expended in producing them (or, at any rate, a portion of their cost) will be expended outside the country. Therefore the exchange of merchandise for local manufactures is more beneficial to the economy than exchange for foreign manufactures; and the exchange of merchandise for manufactures closer to foods, namely those capable of satisfying the most widespread and common comforts, is more useful than exchanges for manufactures which satisfy only the most refined tastes.

Here it is useful to consider how luxury expenditure is proportional to the inequality of goods and ranks. So, we may assert that where wealth is concentrated in a few hands, the influence of the expenditure of those few is correspondingly limited. For when some product originates from a very few people, every transaction involving this product must necessarily depend on another, prior transaction, and that on yet another, even earlier transaction, so that ultimately everything depends on those original few owners. So, however great we suppose the expenditure of those few to be, the whole process will inevitably reflect this initial limitation. As the number of owners of goods increases, however, so the influence of luxury immediately spreads because the spontaneous and independent expenditure of these many owners increases. Thus, in the time-lag between production and reproduction, there will be a smaller number of citizens performing a smaller number of actions in the former case than in the latter; and, as a further result, when external trade is limited and restrained the goods themselves will have a lower value.

Someone might say at this point: if all the lands were divided equally among everyone, then the amount of work done would fall as much as it would if all the lands belonged to just one man. My reply is that it is not necessary to enquire here into how true that is; but, in the first place, this equal distribution of lands is an impossibility, as we showed in Part 2;[1] and in the second place, if we were to find that the effects of these two extreme causes were the same, that might lead us (if I did not fear to presume upon my reader's time and patience by setting off into excessively abstract theorising) to search out that way of distributing lands which would produce the maximum number of useful and productive actions,

---

[1] Beccaria's reference is to §10 in which he argues against the feudal system of entails (*fidecommissari/fidecommessi*) and mainmorts as artificially holding down the value of land and of agricultural produce. Only where there is freedom of trade in land and produce is it worth engaging in agriculture, and where it is worth engaging in agriculture, large landowners will benefit from economies of scale.

that is to say, to search out the proportion which ought to hold between the number of landowners and the number of the nation's other inhabitants, supposing them all to be engaged in trade or work of some sort. I shall merely note that the solution to the problem should presumably be that there ought to be as many landowners as suffice to be counted as many times over relative to the population as a whole as the produce of the lands can be counted relative to the maximum amount of all the efforts not merely which are made, but which could be made, between one harvest and the next, so that, as the lands are brought closer to their maximum productivity, a better distribution will be reached. But all that is not to our present purpose or within the limitations of an elementary course.

Restricting ourselves to the most obvious truths which remain to be set out about luxury, we may say, in the second place, that since there are very sharp dividing-lines (not to say gulfs) between the different social classes, and since people's rank and social standing are determined not only on the basis of the material goods they possess, but also on that of their breeding, birth and other political relations, it follows that the upbringing people receive, their passions and habits, will vary not only according to their wealth but also according to their social position. As a result, it is a noticeable phenomenon that a person's tendency to luxury is the more marked the greater the distance that separates his condition and that immediately above and immediately below. For the desire to stand out and the choices of our pleasures take place in our imitative soul, which is seduced by the example of others, and they are determined by the comparisons we make with the situations of our various fellow citizens. Now, those who are set at some distance above us, or who are humbled below us, do not strike so immediately at our imagination, nor are we concerned to take account of them because they only rarely enter into our sphere of activity, unlike those who are immediately above or below us. So our efforts go into getting on a par with the apparent happiness of the former and to raise ourselves above the latter. Hence, once the highest class in a society is directed towards spending on luxuries that are most conducive to the economic advantage of the state, all the other classes, by a retrograde movement, follow the example, simply by assimilating themselves to the movements and directions of the first.[2]

§35. In view of what has already been said it would be a waste of time to go into details and to examine one by one how the different sorts of luxury expenditure help or hinder the economy of the state. It is only worth pausing for a moment here to examine whether the practices which many mean and melancholy souls would like to introduce would not be diametrically opposed to the end for which they would be advocated. The riches of states arise from nothing other than the work of individuals, and the work of individuals has to be paid for; but men are reluctant to make such payments unless they can convert them into the means for enjoying those things which most satisfy them. Moreover, a man will not work except in proportion to the immediate reward that he hopes to gain from it; and the rewards of this work are distributed as a result of the spending of the rich, that is to say, of those who own more than is necessary for physical survival. The harsher the measures, the smaller will be the spending of these rich people and hence the rewards for the work that is done, and so much the smaller will be the means for converting the payment for it into satisfactions. Therefore, even work and expenditure on the land will diminish, and as a result so will production; therefore the riches, for the conservation and increase of which the measures were called for, will be reduced. Hence, to make perceptible and general progress in getting rid of the pernicious expenditure, which is all that is wanted for the economic aims of the state, the example that the highest classes of society closest to the sovereign can give will suffice, as will freedom of trade, which will convert a large proportion of the sterile expenditure into productive expenditure.

---

[2] Beccaria's imagery in this passage is derived from ancient astronomical theories according to which each celestial body (social class) has it own sphere, in which it moves unacted on by the others; the 'retrograde' movement is the apparent deflection from a simple easterly trajectory across the sky as a result of either eccentrics or epicycles. Even though the theories were discredited, they provide Beccaria with a concise way of expressing the fact that what causes luxury in the highest social class also causes it, in lesser measure, in the others.

Index

Accademia dei pugni x, xiv, xxxi, xxxiii, 124n
accomplices, 95–6
 discovering by use of torture, 44
acquittal, 73–4
Addison, Joseph 123n
adultery, 79–81
age, 154
d'Alembert, Jean-Baptiste Le Rond, xxxiii, xlii, 121, 122, 125
 Elements of Philosophy, xxxiii, 115, 122
 Letter to (Beccaria), xliv, 115–17
 On the Destruction of the Jesuits in France, xxxiii, 116
 Preface to the *Encyclopaedia*, xxxiii, 115, 122
Alexander the Great, 136
Alexandria, 136, 137
amnesties, 111
animals, 145
aristocracy, x–xi, xiii
armed combat, 41
Arouet, François Marie *see* Voltaire
assessors, 35
associationism, xiv
asylum, places of, 92
Aubert, Giuseppi, xli, xlii, xliii, xlv
Austrian Succession, War of (1740–48), x
awards, public, 109

Bacon, Francis, Viscount Verulam, xix, xxxiii, 1, 124, 138

banishment, 56–7, 58–9
bank, 91
bankrupt, fraudulent or innocent, 89–90
Barbarousness and the Civilisation of Nations and on the Savage State of Man, Reflections on the (Beccaria) xix, xxix–xxx, 141–7
Beccaria, Cesare
 biographical details, xi, xxxi–xxxii
 Edizione Nazionale, xliii, xliv
 influence of Pietro Verri on, xi–xvi, xli
 intellectual, social and political context, ix–xxx
 lectures (1769–70), *see Elements of Political Economy* on the Supreme Council of the Economy, xiv, xxxii
 works, *see under titles*
Beccaria, Giulia (his daughter), xi, xxxi
Beccaria, Giulio (his son), xxxii
Belgioioso, Antonia, Countess della Somaglia xxxiii, 126
Bentham, Jeremy, xvi–xvii, xviii, xx, xxvii, xxx
betrayal, 93–4, 95
bibliographical notes, xlvi–xlx
Biffi, Conte Giambattista, xxxii
bills of exchange, 137
biographical glossary, xxxiii–xl
Biumi, Giuseppi, xliii
Blasco, Teresa (Beccaria's wife), xi, xxxi

Index

Index

Index

Index

Index

virtue and vice
  classes of, 4–6
  relative nature of, 20
Visconti, Count, 124
Voltaire, *Commentary* on *Crimes and Punishments* (Beccaria), xxix, xl

War, 146
wealth, circulation of, 165–9
wheel, 64
will, 41

general, 17, 66, 70, 154
witchcraft, 32–3
witchhunts, 99
witnesses, 32–3
Woolf, Stuart, xlviii

Xenophon, 139

Young, D. B., xlviii

Zarone, Giuseppi, xlviii

Cambridge Texts in the History of Political Thought

Titles published in the series thus far

Aristotle *The Politics and The Constitution of Athens* (edited by Stephen Everson)
　o 521 48400 6 paperback
Arnold *Culture and Anarchy and other writings* (edited by Stefan Collini)
　o 521 37796 x paperback
Astell *Political Writings* (edited by Patricia Springborg)
　o 521 42845 9 paperback
Augustine *The City of God against the Pagans* (edited by R.W. Dyson)
　o 521 46843 4 paperback
Austin *The Province of Jurisprudence Determined* (edited by Wilfrid E. Rumble)
　o 521 44756 9 paperback
Bacon *The History of the Reign of King Henry VII* (edited by Brian Vickers)
　o 521 58663 1 paperback
Bakunin *Statism and Anarchy* (edited by Marshall Shatz)
　o 521 36973 8 paperback
Baxter *Holy Commonwealth* (edited by William Lamont)
　o 521 40580 7 paperback
Bayle *Political Writings* (edited by Sally L. Jenkinson)
　o 521 47677 1 paperback
Beccaria *On Crimes and Punishments and other writings* (edited by Richard Bellamy)
　o 521 47982 7 paperback
Bentham *Fragment on Government* (introduction by Ross Harrison)
　o 521 35929 5 paperback
Bernstein *The Preconditions of Socialism* (edited by Henry Tudor)
　o 521 39808 8 paperback
Bodin *On Sovereignty* (edited by Julian H. Franklin)
　o 521 34992 3 paperback
Bolingbroke *Political Writings* (edited by David Armitage)
　o 521 58697 6 paperback
Bossuet *Politics Drawn from the Very Words of Holy Scripture*
(edited by Patrick Riley)
　o 521 36807 3 paperback
The British Idealists (edited by David Boucher)
　o 521 45951 6 paperback
Burke *Pre-Revolutionary Writings* (edited by Ian Harris)
　o 521 36800 6 paperback
Christine De Pizan *The Book of the Body Politic* (edited by Kate Langdon Forhan)
　o 521 42259 o paperback
Cicero *On Duties* (edited by M. T. Griffin and E. M. Atkins)
　o 521 34835 8 paperback
Cicero *On the Commonwealth and On the Laws* (edited by James E. G. Zetzel)
　o 521 45959 1 paperback
Comte *Early Political Writings* (edited by H. S. Jones)
　o 521 46923 6 paperback
Conciliarism and Papalism (edited by J. H. Burns and Thomas M. Izbicki)
　o 521 47674 7 paperback
Constant *Political Writings* (edited by Biancamaria Fontana)
　o 521 31632 4 paperback
Dante *Monarchy* (edited by Prue Shaw)
　o 521 56781 5 paperback

Diderot *Political Writings* (edited by John Hope Mason and Robert Wokler)
0 521 36911 8 paperback
The Dutch Revolt (edited by Martin van Gelderen)
0 521 39809 6 paperback
Early Greek Political Thought from Homer to the Sophists
(edited by Michael Gagarin and Paul Woodruff)
0 521 43768 7 paperback
The Early Political Writings of the German Romantics
(edited by Frederick C. Beiser)
0 521 44951 0 paperback
The English Levellers (edited by Andrew Sharp)
0 521 62511 4 paperback
Erasmus *The Education of a Christian Prince* (edited by Lisa Jardine)
0 521 58811 1 paperback
Fenelon *Telemachus* (edited by Patrick Riley)
0 521 45662 2 paperback
Ferguson *An Essay on the History of Civil Society* (edited by Fania Oz-Salzberger)
0 521 44736 4 paperback
Filmer *Patriarcha and Other Writings* (edited by Johann P. Sommerville)
0 521 39903 3 paperback
Fletcher *Political Works* (edited by John Robertson)
0 521 43994 9 paperback
Sir John Fortescue *On the Laws and Governance of England*
(edited by Shelley Lockwood)
0 521 58996 7 paperback
Fourier *The Theory of the Four Movements* (edited by Gareth Stedman Jones and
Ian Patterson)
0 521 35693 8 paperback
Gramsci *Pre-Prison Writings* (edited by Richard Bellamy)
0 521 42307 4 paperback
Guicciardini *Dialogue on the Government of Florence* (edited by Alison Brown)
0 521 45623 1 paperback
Harrington *The Commonwealth of Oceana* and *A System of Politics*
(edited by J. G. A. Pocock)
0 521 42329 5 paperback
Hegel *Elements of the Philosophy of Right* (edited by Allen W. Wood and
H. B. Nisbet)
0 521 34888 9 paperback
Hegel *Political Writings* (edited by Laurence Dickey and H. B. Nisbet)
0 521 45979 3 paperback
Hobbes *On the Citizen* (edited by Michael Silverthorne and Richard Tuck)
0 521 43780 6 paperback
Hobbes *Leviathan* (edited by Richard Tuck)
0 521 56797 1 paperback
Hobhouse *Liberalism and Other Writings* (edited by James Meadowcroft)
0 521 43726 1 paperback
Hooker *Of the Laws of Ecclesiastical Polity* (edited by A. S. McGrade)
0 521 37908 3 paperback
Hume *Political Essays* (edited by Knud Haakonssen)
0 521 46639 3 paperback
King James VI and I *Political Writings* (edited by Johann P. Sommerville)

(edited by A. S. McGrade and John Kilcullen)
   0 521 35803 5 paperback
William of Ockham *A Letter to the Friars Minor and other writings*
(edited by A. S. McGrade and John Kilcullen)
   0 521 35804 3 paperback
Wollstonecraft *A Vindication of the Rights of Men* and *A Vindication of the Rights of Woman* (edited by Sylvana Tomaselli)
   0 521 43633 8 paperback

CPSIA information can be obtained
at www.ICGtesting.com
Printed in the USA
LVHW04s2321290618
582304LV00001B/71/P